MODI'S GOVERNANCE TRIUMPH

MODI'S GOVERNANCE TRIUMPH

Reshaping India's Path to Prosperity

Tarun Chugh

ink | OCCAM

ISBN: 978-93-92209-97-0

First published in India 2024
This edition published 2024

BluOne Ink Pvt. Ltd
A-76, 2nd Floor, Sector 136, Noida
Uttar Pradesh 201301
www.bluone.ink
publisher@bluone.ink

Printed and bound in India by Thomson Press India Ltd.

ink | OCCAM

To my late father, Shri Banarasi Das Chugh

Contents

Contents

Jagat Prakash Nadda
National President

Bharatiya Janata Party

Date: 12th December, 2023

Message

India's growth, transformation, and heightened standing on the international stage is a transformative tale that merits acquaintance by a broad audience. The book 'Modi's Governance Triumph' by Shri Tarun Chugh, a colleague and astute observer, encapsulates the essence of this transformation. It narrates a tale of leadership that resonates deeply in today's global tapestry, where challenges abound, and the need for visionary leadership is paramount.

This book stands as a testament to the nation's journey towards prosperity. Its meticulous analysis, supported by thorough research and an objective perspective, unveils the human side of governance. The book is enriched with stories of how PM Modi's policies have touched lives, uplifted communities, and driven India towards a brighter future.

As I reflect on the book, I am reminded of the resilience and spirit of India, particularly in these times of global unrest and uncertainty. PM Modi's leadership, characterised by the 'People First' approach, has been a beacon of hope and progress. This book allows us to delve deeper into this approach, exploring how it transcends beyond mere political rhetoric and becomes the backbone of impactful governance.

Having had the privilege of working with Prime Minister Modi in various capacities, I can personally say that this book adeptly captures the essence of PM Modi's unwavering commitment to the welfare of all citizens, particularly those who have been historically marginalized. Additionally, it provides insights into how PM Modi played a pivotal role in elevating India as the voice of the Global South, ensuring that the African Union joined the G20 in record time during the Leaders' Summit in New Delhi. His contributions in international forums, such as the G7, G20, Quad, and more, underscore India's role as a reliable partner in addressing global challenges.

6-A, Deendayal Upadhyay Marg, New Delhi-110 002 | Phone: 011-23500000

"Modi's Governance Triumph" does not merely offer a basic analysis of political strategies; rather, it serves as a source of inspiration and enlightenment. It invites readers to delve into the complexities of India's political landscape and celebrate the nation's triumphs under PM Modi's leadership. The book provides a comprehensive understanding of how PM Modi's governance has not only reshaped India's trajectory within its borders but also on the global stage.

The book "Modi's Governance Triumph" is a succinct yet substantive effort aimed at elucidating Prime Minister Modi's governance and its consequential impact on the people of India. I extend my heartfelt congratulations to Shri Tarun Chugh and the esteemed publisher responsible for bringing forth this insightful contribution. I am confident that "Modi's Governance Triumph" will indeed prove to be a commendable addition to the literary landscape.

Your

(Jagat Prakash Nadda)

Prelude

The scope of my political work and engagement often leaves me with scarce moments to indulge in leisurely reading or writing. Nonetheless, my deep-seated interest in literature and the values instilled in me by the Rashtriya Swayamsevak Sangh compel me to delve into various books, articles, and magazines whenever I can spare a moment.

In an extremely vast and diverse country like India, where the political landscape is multifaceted, it is essential to stay informed about the dynamic social, political, and economic changes unfolding across the nation every passing day. This constant need for awareness has led me to cultivate a habit of reading and documenting my thoughts on a wide range of crucial subjects.

Recently, I had the opportunity to compile these notes into a cohesive document for publication. As I sifted through my accumulated material, I couldn't help but notice a recurring theme—the profound impact of Prime Minister Shri Narendra Modi ji on contemporary socio-political discourse.

Prime Minister Modi ji's influence is undeniable, transcending political affiliations and commanding attention on not just national but also an international scale. As a member of both the Sangh and the BJP, as well as a conscientious citizen of a democratic society, I have witnessed first-hand the transformative changes ushered in under his leadership. The PM has steered India towards unprecedented progress across social, economic, cultural, and scientific realms. He has revitalized our nation, restoring its confidence and igniting a spirit of innovation and resilience.

Today, India stands at the cusp of greatness, propelled by a wave of ambitious initiatives and bold reforms. On the one hand, we have constructed a grand Ram temple, and on the other, one of the world's largest solar power plants has been established in Rewa (MP). From monumental infrastructure projects to ground-breaking scientific endeavours, we are charting a path towards a brighter future under PM Modi ji's visionary guidance. In addition to the construction of the Kashi Vishwanath Corridor, a satellite dedicated to the study of black holes has been launched. While monumental symbols like 'The Statue of Unity' and 'Statue of Oneness' stand tall, multipurpose modern centres such as 'Bharat Mandapam' and 'Yashobhoomi' have been established. India is forging ahead, laying an average of 40 kilometres of new roads every day, having established 7 new IITs and opened 74 new airports in the past 10 years. Bold decisions like the integration of banks, the abrogation of Article 370, the enactment of the triple talaq law, the implementation of the GST, and the initiation of the Agniveer Yojana have been undertaken. As we celebrate our rich heritage and embrace cutting-edge technologies, our PM is bridging the gap between tradition and modernity, fostering a harmonious synthesis of ancient wisdom and contemporary innovation. Moreover, Shri Narendra Modi ji's pragmatic approach extends beyond national boundaries, positioning India as a global leader in areas such as renewable energy, climate action, and sustainable development.

I am confident that with collective effort and determination, we will overcome the challenges ahead and realize our vision of a prosperous and inclusive India by 2047.

I express my heartfelt gratitude to my friends Sumeet Bhasin ji and Hemant Mehra ji as well as my colleagues Lovepreet Singh ji, Rohan Mahajan ji, Naresh Ji, and Aryaman ji for their unwavering support throughout this intellectual journey. Special thanks are also due to Tarsem Kumar ji, whose invaluable assistance played a crucial role in bringing all the pieces together. I am sincerely grateful to all those who have supported me and contributed to the compilation of this work. While every effort has been made to ensure accuracy, I humbly apologize for any oversights that may have occurred.

Introduction

India now is at the centre stage of the world order. Indian voice is most sought after at the global forum. The world without India cannot be imagined. India is the hope of the world. World peace needs Indian patronage. The fight against global hunger is led by India. The fightback against climate change has an Indian script. India is now the hope of the Global South. It has become the saviour for small nations trapped in debt by cunning economic imperial powers. India is the first responder to disasters in any part of the world. India is the hope for global humanity to live in peace with nature.

Within the country, India is now politically stable. The people gave two decisive mandates for stable governments at the Centre – first in 2014 and then in 2019. The people became aware of the benefits of a stable government and firm leadership. Politics of stability is now a new normal. The days of political instability are over. Politics is now an engine of good governance. The government works for the well-being of the people. Governance is about working towards making democracy work as a government of the people, for the people and by the people. Indian democracy is now cruising on the path of accelerated upliftment of poor people, protection of the middle class and respect for wealth creators. The resources of the country are spent to protect the interests of the most vulnerable and to make the country self-reliant in all spheres. India is also now a crucial part of the global supply chains.

The turnaround in the India story took place under the stewardship of Narendra Modi, who, in his two terms as prime minister, has brought about a definitive change in the politics of the country to make governance visible and benign for all sections of the people. The Narendra Modi model of politics and governance needs deeper analysis to understand the science and art of statecraft. There is a method leading to perfection in the true spirit of science. There is a connect with the people, ensuring their participation in every endeavour of governance in the true spirit of the art. This coexistence of science and art of politics and governance in the country spurred extraordinary scaling up of collective efforts of all the stakeholders to take India into the top league in the global community in a short span of time.

There is a method in the Modi way of politics; there is a process in his governance model. Challenges are met as part of the methodical model of governance with Modi at the helm. There have been no signs of panic even in the face of extreme adversity of unknown pedigree and proportions, as revealed by the coronavirus. Perseverance is the hallmark of the Modi path of governance. With the people occupying the centre stage of the Modi path of governance, the best expertise is heard with patience and given free hands to deal with the situation while the prime minister gives the necessary cover.

This art of governance saw India through the tough times of the pandemic. The leadership acted with agility to opt for a national lockdown to minimize harm to the people and also find time for scientists to work on the response mechanism. The global community hailed the Indian way of dealing with the pandemic of the century. Yet, India didn't lose sight of the responsibility towards global humanity enshrined in the Indian philosophy of *vasudhaiva kutumbakam* (the world is one family). That the world is one village was truly seen in reality as the Indian-made medicines and vaccines reached all corners of the world, not to leave the small islands in the Caribbean and the Pacific, besides caring for the poor nations, who may not have afforded the costly jabs made by the multinational corporations.

Several working groups formed by the Central government to deal with the situations arising out of the pandemic and the Union ministers reaching out to cross-sections of the stakeholders, from the district magistrates to the heads of the zila panchayats and even further down the administrative units, remain the unprecedented intervention of the Modi government to make democracy function in its true spirit. This institutionalized the 'people first' approach to governance under the leadership of Modi.

The centrality of the people in the statecraft with empathy has defined the Modi style of governance. Modi witnessed the attempt of Chandrayaan-2 to land the Rover Vikram on the Moon. The scientists were predictably tense, and unfortunately, the mission failed. Modi's presence reassured the scientists at the Indian Space Research Organisation (ISRO) that disappointments should remain temporary, and they must not lose time to begin working on the Chandrayaan-3 mission. The Modi path to governance accords a place of eminence to scientists in the country. Once more, the prime minister joined the ISRO scientists virtually from Johannesburg to witness the last few minutes of the Chandrayaan-3 mission's landing on the Moon. This time Modi shared the joys of the scientists as India achieved the feat of becoming the first country in the world to land a mission at the South Pole of the Moon. Perseverance and unwavering faith in the ability of the scientists brought cheers not just to the people of the country but across the world. Modi knew the significance of the moment, and he rightly dedicated the achievement of India to global humanity. This philosophy of 'Vasudhev Kutumbakam' is a working principle of the world view of the Modi path of governance.

The leadership of more than a billion people in the 21st century must be decisive. India can take its rightful position in the global order only if the leadership is firm in decision-making while also being visionary and far-sighted. The leadership must find solutions that are long-lasting. Before Modi took charge of the country, bomb blasts and terror attacks were commonplace. Infiltration in Jammu and Kashmir was unabated. Secessionist forces were at their peak. Separatists in the Kashmir Valley ran the show. It was a fait accompli for the people to live in the shadow of terror.

But the response of the Modi path of governance sent shivers down the spines of the sponsors of terror. The Uri surgical strike and the Balakot air strike sent the message across the border that the cost of exporting terrorism could be beyond the paying capacity of Pakistan. The terror launch pads were destroyed. Terrorists were eliminated. Infiltration episodes were turned off. The Kashmir Valley forgot the episodes of stone pelting. The decision to demonetize dried up the fake currency supply line of the terrorists. The ground was made ready in the Kashmir Valley to look into a future of peace and tranquillity. The future of Kashmir is in real integration with the country, and the artificial barrier in the form of Article 370 was also blown to smithereens in 2019, soon after the Bharatiya Janata Party bagged their second mandate with a record number of Lok Sabha seats.

Seven decades of living with an artificial barrier, which had bonded the fate of the people in Jammu and Kashmir to the two families of Abdullahs and Muftis, while denying the rights to women, the downtrodden, tribe groups, scheduled castes gave way to a new dawn. Tricolour dots the skyline in the Kashmir Valley now. The people in the Valley wholeheartedly celebrate the Independence Day celebrations. They joyously and voluntarily took the oath of 'paanch pran' given by Modi to make India a developed nation by 2047, when the country would celebrate the centenary of Independence.

The world also became aware of the true picture of Jammu and Kashmir after the abrogation of Article 370. The successful hosting of the tourism summit during the G20 was applauded by world leaders. Businesses in the Valley are flourishing amid a record inflow of tourists. Foreign tourists are also making a beeline to the Valley. The people now realize that the gains after the abrogation of Article 370 have been extraordinary. Now, there is no sympathy for the erstwhile ruling political families. The Modi path of governance has no place for dynasts, and this helped the leadership to take people's views into account in Jammu and Kashmir, which helped in achieving a lasting solution.

The Modi path to governance is essentially built on the principles of sustainable development. India remains steadfast in fulfilling its commitments to the sustainable development goals (SDGs). Modi's LiFE articulation also calls for a sustainable lifestyle in sync with nature. With International Solar Alliance hosted in the country, India has taken a lead in the global clean energy transition. Also, India is a part of solutions to climate challenge.

At the same time, India, with Modi at the helm, exhibited the pinnacle of democratic functioning by giving the charge of the G20 presidency to the people of the country. He rightly said in the 104th episode of *Mann Ki Baat*, the monthly radio broadcast, that the Indian G20 presidency essentially became a people's presidency. The people's participation in several initiatives of the government under the watch of Modi became runaway successes. Revival of the water bodies, sanitation, cleaning of the mountains, making India TB-free, vocal for local to promote the handicraft industry and others have been highly successful because of the people's participation.

Inclusive development is at the core of the Modi path of governance. The unequivocal commitment to mainstream the stakeholders of the economy, who were kept on the margins, paid rich dividends as the financial inclusion through Jan Dhan Yojna changed the fortunes of millions of workers in the unorganized sector. The Aadhaar architecture for financial inclusion gave the government the scale and speed to deliver welfare benefits to the people. This helped in scripting a corruption-free governance, which has been making a deep impact on the delivery of public services to the last mile. The middlemen are eliminated. The benefits are directly going to the beneficiaries. The effort is being replicated in the healthcare sector by drastically cutting the cost of medicines as well as medical equipment to save on the pocket expenditure of the people. The Modi path of governance has ensured that the people now have disposable income to spend on their aspirational needs, including imparting education of choice to the children, as well as gaining skills to climb the socio-economic ladder.

At the core of the Modi path to governance lies the undiluted commitment of 'India First, Nation First'. Nothing can come in the way of the pursuit of national interests. The abiding commitment is to the national interests. The world also took note of India's firm resolve to pursue the national interest in the wake of the outbreak of the Russia–Ukraine conflict. India didn't take sides. The Indian voice was only for peace, as Modi told the Russian president Vladimir Putin that 'this is not an era of war'. India espoused the cause of diplomacy. India didn't take sides and kept the voices of reason strong by calling upon both sides to come to the negotiating table. Such visionary leadership has been exceptional on the world stage.

1

Modi Wages War against Poverty

Prime Minister Narendra Modi interacting with beneficiaries of the Ayushman Bharat scheme in Dhar, Madhya Pradesh

Since the first election in the country, eliminating poverty has always been at the centre stage of the promises of political parties. The Congress famously gave the slogan 'Garibi Hatao' when the former prime minister Indira Gandhi was faced with rising unpopularity because of the excesses committed by her during the Emergency. Political parties consistently placed the poor at the forefront of their electoral promises. But their conditions wouldn't improve; at best, some cosmetic changes would be carried out by the Congress governments at the Centre and the states to show that the party really was concerned about the situations of the poor.

The former prime minister Rajiv Gandhi admitted in an oft-quoted remark that one rupee sent by New Delhi for the wellbeing of the poor reduces to fifteen paise by the time it reaches the beneficiaries. This was an admission of the monumental scale of corruption in the schemes run for the wellbeing of the poor in the country. The Congress governments were clueless about how to deal with the leakages in the implementation of government schemes.

Corruption and Congress governments shared symbiotic relations. They needed each other to survive. Hoarding and black marketeering of essential goods and items of daily needs were the norms of the Congress government.

During the tenure of the United Progressive Alliance (UPA), led by the former prime minister Manmohan Singh, the country saw two instances of rampant corruption in the implementation of government schemes. The first was revealed by the performance audit of the Mahatma Gandhi National Rural Employment Guarantee Scheme (MGNREGS) by the Comptroller and Auditor General (CAG). It was revealed that funds for the scheme sent by the Centre were being siphoned off by vested interests and work was being done only on paper. Under the UPA government, the MGNREGS became synonymous with corruption. Instead of genuinely poor rural folks availing the guaranteed man-days of work, babus, politicians and contractors usurped the benefits, and the condition of the poor never improved.

The UPA government also announced a loan-waiver scheme for farmers. The CAG report later revealed that the money sent by the Centre was being usurped by vested interests and genuine beneficiaries such as farmers were bereft of their dues even as they continued to bear the weight of growing debt burden. In addition, the farmers faced black marketing of fertilizers, so they took out loans to buy diesel to run pumping sets to irrigate their farmland. The farmers were stuck in the cobweb of high debt, mounting input costs and lack of market to sell their produces for remunerative prices. Under the watch of the UPA government, a large number of farmers slipped into the poverty trap and suicides committed by them regularly grabbed the national headlines.

It was in the backdrop of the abundant failure of the Congress in its slogan and oft-repeated promise of 'Garibi Hatao' that Prime Minister Narendra Modi was given the mandate by the poor by overwhelmingly voting for the Bharatiya Janata Party (BJP) and his leadership in the 2014 Lok Sabha elections. The poor saw hope in PM Modi. They trusted in the leadership of PM Modi after knowing the work he did for the upliftment of the poor in Gujarat, where he headed the government as the chief minister more than a decade ago. The achievements of the Modi government in Gujarat in making the poor self-dependent and increasing their income had reached all corners of the country.

During the 2014 Lok Sabha elections, people in several states told visiting journalists that poverty had reduced in Gujarat by a huge margin. The fast-paced industrialization of Gujarat, along with a massive scale of employment generation by the manufacturing sector, had created a positive image of Gujarat under Modi, which gave a ray of hope to the people across the country. Modi meant hope for the people. Words spoken by Modi were believed by the people. Across the country, people welcomed Modi by expressing their undiluted affection, not seen for decades in the country.

The arrival of Modi on the national scene took place at a time when Delhi had become a hub of protests. Jantar Mantar in New Delhi was brimming with protestors of all hues. The Ram Lila ground frequently hosted protestors. It looked as if there was an anarchy in the country, and the people had all been taking trains and buses to reach Delhi to protest. The headlines were full of negative news of scams in ministries at scales that stunned even the wild imagination of the people. Corruption hurts the poor the most. This has been established by social scientists in their research papers across the world. National resources, which could have been deployed to improve the conditions of the poor, were diverted to benefit vested interests during the UPA government. India even reported incidents of hunger. Children of the poor dropped out of schools in large number. Schools in rural, semi-urban and even urban areas were without basic facilities. Girls dropped out of schools more because of lack of toilet facilities, but the government paid no attention to visible signs of distress among the poor.

'Antyodaya' is the guiding philosophy of the BJP. The upliftment of the last person in the ladder – the rise of the last (antyodaya) – was at the core of Pandit Deen Dayal Upadhyay's political philosophy. This runs in the vein of the BJP and the party workers. For the BJP, politics is not an instrument to grab power; it is a means to serve the people. The BJP, wedded to the philosophy of Pandit Deen Dayal Upadhyay, seeks power to work for the betterment of the people. Service to society is the mantra that guides the BJP.

Atal Bihari Vajpayee, the first prime minister from among the BJP ranks, revealed glimpses of the political philosophy of BJP in action when he headed the National Democratic Alliance (NDA) government at the Centre from 1998 to 2004. People realized that the Vajpayee government was not making promises in the air but was laying the groundwork, with vision and action, to eradicate poverty and rural backwardness. Swarojgar Yojna, which preceded the MGNREGS, was such an intervention on the part of the Vajpayee government to help the poor meet the immediate need for employment even while the long-term measures in the form of the Pradhan Mantri Grameen Sadak Yojna (PMGSY) were being executed to help rural parts of the country come closer to urban centres and improve economic activities.

Studies have shown that Swarojgar Yojna and the PMGSY have proven to be catalysts for the revival of the rural economy as well as helping the poor gain social and economic empowerment. The Vajpayee government brought rural India to the centre stage of policy-making of the government. Unlike the UPA government, which dealt with rural India with contempt, the BJP has shown with action that the party believes in the core mantra that each part of the country must partake in the development process. This alone can guarantee sustainable development. This also explains the core mantra of '*sabka vikas*' given by PM Modi.

It's against this backdrop that the people of the country welcomed the arrival of Modi on the national scene. They recalled the extraordinary work done by the Vajpayee government in a short spell of time. People believed that Modi would deliver, on a grand scale, the foundation laid by Vajpayee for the country. They knew that the BJP meant service to the people. And it is unconditional service. The BJP doesn't set conditions for a service to the people, unlike other political parties, which rely on and nurture vote banks. Only empowered people can ensure a strong nation. Thus, the 'Nation First' mantra of the BJP essentially enshrines the life breath of the 'People First' mantra. It is this clarity that guides the BJP, and this has been put into action with extraordinary clarity and vision by PM Modi in his two terms as the prime minister of the country.

The 'People First' approach of the BJP found the finest fulfilment in the statecraft of PM Modi. The foundation was laid by eliminating even the remotest scope of corruption. Thus, a graft-free edifice of the Modi government was built on the assertion of '*na khaunga, na khane dunga*' right from the ramparts of the Red Fort. PM Modi drew a bold line of his statecraft that scorched any possibilities of corruption. This helped in the elimination of middlemen from several Central schemes.

No palm needs to be greased for availing benefits from the Central government. To achieve this, the Modi government needed a transparent delivery architecture. The JAM (Jan Dhan Yojna, Aadhaar and Mobile) trinity became the foundation of a graft-free, transparent delivery mechanism of the Central government. PM Modi built on the strong foundation laid by the Vajpayee government. The mobile revolution in the country is credited to Vajpayee. It was the visionary leadership of Vajpayee that accelerated telecommunication connectivity in the country. Affordable technology and cheapest telecom tariff ensured that even the poorest in the country were equipped with a mobile handset.

Financial inclusion was an unfulfilled aspiration of several million people in the country. Millions of people, for want of bank access, were exposed to moneylenders and unscrupulous elements who ran chit funds and deposit schemes in the country. The poor lost their money to such financial scamsters in the country. The dailies regularly came up with headlines about the poor people in the country losing their hard-earned money to the unorganized deposit schemes run by unapproved operators. Even the likes of Manmohan Singh, who is an economist, could not ensure financial inclusion of millions of people.

Hardworking daily wagers who put up stalls on the pavements were forced to carry cash at great risk of losing it to anti-social elements. Millions of people in the country were deprived of banking credits in the formal sector because of which they were forced to take loans from moneylenders at rates that bonded them for life in a debt trap. By the time the UPA government demitted office, rural indebtedness was at a record high. The enterprising, hardworking youth from this section of society could never take part in the formal economy because they were deprived of the banking network.

But PM Modi put the stated philosophy of his statecraft – *sabka vikas* – in action, and it was done through the Jan Dhan bank accounts. Since the launch of the Jan Dhan Yojna on 24 August 2014, more than 48 crore bank accounts have been opened. PM Modi had made the announcement of the Jhan Dhan campaign in his speech from the ramparts of the Red Fort. Within a short span of time, the excluded class became financially included. The first pillar of the JAM trinity had taken a deep foundation. The third pillar of the trinity – Aadhar seeding – was fast-paced with the help of the second pillar – mobile phones. Thus, JAM proved a revolutionary intervention by the Modi government to deliver graft-free welfare schemes to the people with just a click of the mouse.

The JAM trinity would soon become the cornerstone of the Modi statecraft, which would then be hailed globally for its fast-paced inclusive development. The ease of execution of government schemes was achieved because of the JAM trinity, in which transparency was also guaranteed. The middlemen were kicked out. The trust of the people in the delivery capabilities of the government was now absolute. The impact became visible on the ground.

Not only the national media but even the international media gave accounts of the toilets built in the country by the time the country went to the next Lok Sabha elections in 2019. Toilets brought gender justice, which was never thought of, and also ensured improvement in health parameters, which in turn cut down the out-of-pocket expenditure of the people in availing treatments for several ailments. The Modi statecraft had its heart beating for Antyodaya, and the administration was sensitive to the needs of the downtrodden in the country.

India, unfortunately, could not avoid importing the coronavirus. The pandemic soon spread across the country. PM Modi acted swiftly to safeguard the population by clamping a national lockdown. The first thought to flash in PM Modi's mind was the risk to the poor. He was aware of the threat of hunger, so he ensured food security through PM Garib Kalyan Yojna. In a bold move with no parallel anywhere in the world, PM Garib Kalyan Yojna was announced for 80 crore people, ensuring free food grains to all. This shielded the people from the threat of hunger. In addition, the scheme helped people save on their expenditures, which otherwise would have incurred in buying food items, and spend instead on other needs. This again had visible impact on people's health and nutrition.

The hard work done by the Modi government in uplifting and empowering the poor through Antyodaya hit international headlines when the multidimensional poverty index report was released by the United Nations Development Programme (UNDP) in association with Oxford University. Later, in 2023, the NITI Aayog came out with its own multidimensional poverty index report. The report revealed that the Modi government had indeed moved the mountain of poverty, which had been unmoved for several decades despite loud slogans of 'Garibi Hatao'.

NITI Aayog's report *National Multidimensional Poverty Index: A Progress Review 2023* stated that a record 13.5 crore people had moved out of multidimensional poverty between 2015–16 and 2019–21. The report drew on the findings of the National Family Health Survey (NFHS-5 2019–21). The NITI Aayog report was based on simultaneous deprivations across the three equally weighted dimensions of health, education and standard of living. They are also enshrined in the twelve SDGs, such as nutrition, child and adolescent mortality, maternal health, years of schooling, school attendance, cooking fuel, sanitation, drinking water, electricity, housing, assets and bank accounts.

Now, it may be recalled that the monumental intervention of the Modi government through various schemes made all the changes in the lives of the people. The Ujjwala scheme freed women in the country from kitchen smoke. Mission Indradhanush ensured universal immunisation. Toilets ensured basic hygiene. Pradhan Mantri Jan Arogya Yojna gave access to quality treatment for ailments. Jan Aushadhi ensured that affordable medicines were provided to the people, which drastically reduced prices of medicines in the country. Substantial expansion in hospital infrastructure, including AIIMS, took place. Poshan Abhiyan, which tracks the nutrition level of women and children in the country, provided a meaningful intervention in addressing key concerns of social scientists.

The aspirational districts programme, covering the most backward districts in the country, made interventions in the areas of health, education, nutrition and others by bringing all the stakeholders on a common platform. Now, the aspirational programme has been taken to the block level after encouraging results came in from district levels.

Thus, India was able to register a significant decline of 9.89 percentage points in the number of multidimensionally poor from 24.85 per cent in 2015–16 to 14.96 per cent in 2019–21, with rural areas witnessing the fastest decline in poverty from 32.59 per cent to 19.28 per cent. Urban areas also saw a reduction in poverty from 8.65 per cent to 5.27 per cent making achievements at the national level equally distributed across the country. The positive impact of the Modi craft in giving killer knocks to poverty touched the lives of the people in all the regions of the country.

Uttar Pradesh gained the most as per the report, with the state registering the largest decline in the number of poor as 3.43 crore people came out of multidimensional poverty. The report captured the status of multidimensional poverty in 36 states and union territories and 707 administrative districts. Such an exhaustive and elaborate capture of the impact of the schemes was never seen in the history of independent India. The report of the NITI Aayog was in consonance with international findings.

The fastest reduction in the proportion of multidimensional poor was observed in Uttar Pradesh, Bihar, Madhya Pradesh, Odisha and Rajasthan. The MPI value was halved from 0.117 to 0.066 between 2015–16 and 2019–21. The NITI Aayog report also stated that the intensity of poverty came down from 47 per cent to 44 per cent. PM Modi had been stating at various international fora that India is on course to achieve the SDG targets set by the UN for 2030. Similarly, the NITI Aayog report underlined that India is cruising on the path of achieving the SDGs of reducing multidimensional poverty by at least half, much ahead of the timeline of 2030.

This again demonstrates that the Modi craft, rooting for Antyodaya and following the true philosophy of Pandit Deen Dayal Upadhyay, delivered sustainable and equitable development. This was possible because PM Modi took ownership of several campaigns to address issues of sanitation, nutrition, cooking fuel, financial inclusion, drinking water and electricity. The outcome of the prime minister leading from the front in achieving the aims of the Central interventions was seen in the multidimensional poverty report – all twelve parameters of the MPI reported marked improvements, with programmes like Poshan Abhiyan and Anaemia Mukt Bharat making stellar contributions to reducing deprivations in health and initiatives such as Swachh Bharat Mission (SBM) and Jal Jeevan Mission (JJM) improving sanitation for all. Indeed, 21.8 percentage points improvement in sanitation deprivations were reported in the MPI-based report of the NITI Aayog.

Pradhan Mantri Ujjwala Yojana (PMUY) added 14.6 percentage points improvement in cooking fuel deprivations. Saubhagya, Pradhan Mantri Awas Yojana (PMAY), Pradhan Mantri Jan Dhan Yojana (PMJDY) and Samagra Shiksha also contributed significantly in reducing multidimensional poverty in the country. National and international agencies endorsed that a government committed to the true wellbeing of the poor can indeed reduce poverty in a short span of time. This also explains why people in the country have absolute trust in the leadership of PM Modi. The prime minister is a man of action, and he delivers what he speaks on the ground with measurable outcomes.

2

Modi's *Arthniti*

Prime Minister Narendra Modi while inaugurating several development projects in Jamnagar, Gujarat

Becoming the Fifth Largest Economy

India became the fifth largest economy by moving ahead of the UK. Indian economy is larger than four of the G7 countries. The Indian economy is bigger than the four most industrialized and wealthy nations. The roadmap for India to emerge as the third largest economy in the world has been endorsed by several multilateral institutions as well as global rating agencies. India remains the world's fastest growing major economy. The introduction of the goods and services tax (GST) to ensure 'one nation, one tax' subsumed seventeen major taxes and thirteen cesses, leading to collections growing by 12 per cent in April 2023 to ₹1.87 lakh crore,[1] which was the highest monthly mop-up since the rollout of the landmark taxation reform measure in the country since Independence.

Along with the introduction of the unified payment interface (UPI), the single largest retail payment platform in the country, the taxation reforms as well as digital architecture gave Indian economy fresh legs to run in tough times, which were marred by the coronavirus pandemic. Now, UPI-based payment system is going global with agreements in place with a host of nations such as Nepal, Singapore, the UAE and France. This marks the arrival of the Indian digital economy on the world stage and also boosts easy capital flow to expatriates, businesses and entrepreneurs.

An Atmanirbhar Bharat package of ₹27.1 lakh crore[2] was rolled out by the Modi government to safeguard the Indian economy from the ill-effects of the COVID-19 pandemic. The robust rise in GST collections, increase in capital expenditure outlay and record growth in exports affirmed resilience of the Indian economy, which not only withstood the wrath of the pandemic but also shined on the global stage. The Modi mantra of India First and a caring touch to all sections of society had given an impregnable shield to the Indian economy. The Modi government acted with speed that was not matched by any other in the world. The government's holistic approach since 2014 strengthened the economy and paid rich dividends. The structural reforms initiated by the Modi government strengthened the Indian economy, enabling it to withstand the unprecedented effects of the pandemic.

The India First mantra once more guided Atmanirbhar Bharat and Make in India campaigns to give firm footing to the Indian economy. Production-linked incentive (PLI) schemes were designed and crafted for several sectors to make them globally competitive. The PLI schemes aimed to make domestic manufacturing globally competitive, besides nurturing domestic leaders in the manufacturing sector. The PLI schemes created lakhs of employment opportunities and opened new avenues for the Indian economy to gain growth.

This is reflected in the fact that India, from being a net importer of mobile phones, became a global manufacturing hub. The production of mobile phones has risen from about 60 million[3] in 2014–15 to over 310 million in 2021–22. A record $676.5 billion in goods and services exports was achieved in FY 2021–22.[4] From being an importer of mobiles to $5.5 billion in mobile exports[5] capture the true turnaround of manufacturing in the country.

The Modi government made MSMEs a central focus of its economic policy. The government's emergency credit line guarantee scheme during the COVID pandemic protected more than one crore MSMEs and saved them from possible permanent closure. Moreover, reforms such as revision of MSME definition and changes in labour and environment laws allowed MSMEs to expand their operations and grow. PM Modi has consistently assured the country's wealth creators adequate support in their efforts towards innovation and making India self-reliant. This is reflected in his personal focus and support for the Indian Semiconductor Mission (ISM) and its vision of building a semiconductor and display manufacturing ecosystem in India. India has also emerged as a preferred investment hub under PM Modi's leadership, which is affirmed by record annual FDI inflow of $83.57 billion in fiscal 2021–22.[6]

Total FDI inflow in the 2007–14 period was ₹21 lakh crore[7] and it increased by a whopping 96 per cent to reach ₹42 lakh crore in 2014–22,[8] reaching the highest FDI inflow of ₹6.78 lakh crore in FY 2021–22.

The Modi government also announced a new Foreign Trade Policy to boost Indian exports. It was aligned with the ambition to take India's goods and services exports to a record level. The policy gives impetus to India's aim to rapidly expand the size of the Indian economy. India's agriculture exports touched a historic high of $50 billion.[9]

The impact of the Modi mantra of India First in the management of the Indian economy has been endorsed globally by think tanks who have said that India will remain the world's fastest growing major economy for years to come. High growth will lead to greater resources for the government and allow further expansion of welfare schemes and infrastructure projects; fast growth leads to the creation of new employment opportunities, which in turn will lead to a steady rise in incomes and distribution of benefits of growth to every section of society.

Aatmanirbhar Bharat

Prime Minister Narendra Modi believes in turning adversity into opportunity. He has been able to demonstrate such a rare skill since the Bhuj earthquakes in Gujarat, when he was the chief minister of the state. This again was reflected in the robust economic management by PM Modi after the outbreak of the pandemic. He seized the moment to turn adversity into an opportunity.

The efforts were reflected in all the economic indicators pointing towards India's economic resurgence, as from MSMEs to MNCs, all firms witnessed expansion in output. This contributed to a historic rise in services, manufacturing and exports for the country, putting the Indian economy in a state of resilience. The fact that hiring sentiment remains at an all-time high in many sectors ensures that growth converts to jobs. This is a departure from the jobless growth seen during the time of the Manmohan Singh government at the Centre.

PM Modi gave strong arms to the Indian economy by carrying out reforms with conviction and consensus. It is to the credit of PM Modi that he started a new trend of reforms by personally pushing many structural reforms caught at difficult stages. The cornerstone of the conviction of PM Modi is cooperative federalism, which means that the Centre is encouraging states to voluntarily undertake reforms by incentivizing their efforts. Economists have sought to explain this aspect by attributing the efforts to the nudge principle executed by PM Modi in his economic management as well as spearheading unprecedented reforms in all walks of life.

PM Modi, in his actions, has demonstrated that his government protects interests of all stakeholders of the economy, which helped build a better economy for the country, which in turn is capable of facing future challenges. Introduction of Goods and Services Tax (GST) led to greater formalization of the Indian economy. Besides, a sharp decline in the non-performing assets of the banks and economic offences due to strict action by the government helped the economy become healthy.

The legislative architecture put in place by the Modi government to clean up the legacy mess of the bad loans of the banks salvaged the situation for the Indian banking and corporate sectors.

The indicators turned green in several areas to boost the confidence of the stakeholders in the Indian economy, as India's ease of doing business ranking rose to 63rd in 2019 from 142nd in 2014.[10] Indeed, deep reforms, such as four labour codes, helped achieve the transition. The ease of doing business also helped in 1.67 lakh new companies getting registered in 2021–22,[11] highest ever in a single financial year. The India Inc. also gained confidence as the government cut the corporate tax to 15 per cent from 25 per cent for new domestic manufacturing companies. Besides, the Modi government repealed more than 1,500 laws that were redundant or outdated and acted as impediments in the ease of doing business.[12] The number of steps required for company incorporation decreased from fourteen in 2014 to three in 2022. Direct tax for domestic companies, too, was brought down from 30 per cent to 25 per cent.

Now, the world is looking at India as an attractive destination for investment. Global companies want to establish businesses in India as an endorsement of PM Modi's thrust for transformative governance and economic reforms to enhance the ease of doing business in India. The efforts gave growth wings to existing as well as new businesses and entrepreneurs. They also pitched in by raising their investments and by setting up businesses in India.

Since 2014, rent-seeking and red-tapism have been replaced by a red carpet for investors and industries. The government is not an obstacle in the path of risk-takers but is an active enabler. Entrepreneurs and investors are attracted to India now because of its business-friendly environment. The government is steps ahead to address concerns and redress grievances of businesses. This paradigm shift has been made possible through landmark decisions such as removing retrospective taxation, Angel tax and lowering corporate tax. The National Single Window System now allows obtaining all approvals through a single platform.

PM Modi's mantra of transparency and reducing compliance requirements demonstrates a government that trusts its citizens, which is being reciprocated with the rising number of taxpayers and record tax collections. Similarly, promoting self-regulation, self-certification, computerized random labour inspections and faceless assessment/appeal in taxes has not only dealt a blow to 'Inspector Raj' but also improved compliance. India's efforts to improve the ease of doing business are being acknowledged on the global stage. This is evident in consistent improvement in various international rankings.

India has climbed six places on the World Bank's Logistic Performance Index (LPI) 2023,[13] now ranking 38th in the 139-countries index. This is a strong indicator of India's global positioning, with this development being powered by the government's laser focus on reforms for improving logistics infrastructure through initiatives like PM Gati Shakti and the new National Logistics Policy. The thrust towards greater transparency and a level playing field for MSMEs and small businesses is exemplified by the success of the Government e-Marketplace (GeM) portal, with transactions surpassing ₹4 lakh crore.[14]

Indeed, PM Modi spearheaded a mindset transformation by inculcating a culture of considering entrepreneurs as wealth creators while also making them partners in national development. This has been seen in a historic expansion in the pool of wealth creators, which in turn had a butterfly effect on the economy as resources available to the government went up to roll out welfare and development programmes, while at the same time enabling job creation and higher incomes in the country.

Infrastructure Push

The Indian economy gained strong foundation on the strength of its robust infrastructure, which was boosted by an increase of 500 per cent in road transport and highway budget allocation since 2014. Rural road connectivity has reached 99 per cent coverage and 3.28 lakh km of rural roads have been upgraded since 2014.[15] The PM Gati Shakti Mission to provide multimodal connectivity infrastructure connecting thirty-five Central government departments has acted as a force multiplier in raising the stakes of infrastructure in the Indian economy. The pace of highway construction reached 37 km/day from 12 km/day.[16]

The government also gave a push for faster mobility in the country by committing to the manufacturing of 400 world-class Vande Bharat trains, while twenty-four trains are already operational. Besides, seventy-four airports have been operationalized since 2014 in the country.[17] Crucial infrastructure projects stalled for decades are finally getting completed and opened for use by the public. PM Modi's meticulous monitoring and tracking through the PRAGATI platform proved to be a game changer in giving a push to the execution of the infrastructure projects in the country. The government also ensured that the COVID-19 pandemic did not affect the timely completion of infrastructure projects as PM Modi remained steadfast in his commitment to oversee the creation of new infrastructure for New India.

Some of the landmark achievements are: 2.5 km four-lane concrete road built in twenty-four hours;[18] one-lane 25 km bitumen Solapur–Bijapur road built in twenty-four hours;[19] tallest statue in the world – Statue of Unity; world's highest railway bridge being built – Chenab Bridge; world's longest highway tunnel above 10,000 feet – Atal Tunnel Infrastructure; long-term planning for India's infrastructure needs through PM Gati Shakti Masterplan; ₹100 lakh crore through an integrated platform that ensures efficient use of funds;[20] and last-mile connectivity and multi-modal connectivity improved across India.

Besides, 111 waterways have been declared national waterways under the National Waterways Act 2016. More than 1,537 projects at an estimated cost of around ₹6.5 lakh crore have been identified for implementation under the Sagarmala Programme. The 1,380-km-long

Delhi–Mumbai Expressway is being developed at a cost of ₹96,000 crore and has been partly operational since February 2023.

Farmers First

Prime Minister Narendra Modi has crafted an economic policy for genuine advancement of the economic conditions of the people. Farmers, women, youth, young entrepreneurs and others have felt the caring touch of the Modi arthniti (economics). The abiding philosophy is to expand the Indian economy by firing all engines. The aim is to attain inclusive growth. The objective is prosperity of all. The mantra is India First. A confident India resting on firm feet will take her rightful position in the global order. Thus, the Modi Niti in economy is guided by the foremost goal of taking the third position in the size of the economy in another two decades. This is the hard work being done in the 'Amrit Kal' by PM Modi for India to become a developed nation by the time the country commemorates 100 years of Independence.

Over half the population of the country is dependent on agriculture. Farmers and farm labourers have found the topmost attention of the Modi government. Agriculture budget rose by over 5.6 times[21] to cover the needs of each area of agriculture to ensure that the farmers gain from the remunerative prices of their produces as well as that farming activities become sustainable. As much as ₹93,068 crore have been allocated under the Pradhan Mantri Krishi Sinchai Yojana during 2021–26,[22] while the minimum support price (MSP) witnessed 50 per cent growth.[23] This was done on priority to protect farmers from price distortions.

The India First approach was also seen in the MSP. At the time PM Modi took charge of the country, India was battling high prices of pulses as the government imported lentils from African and East Asian countries. PM Modi called upon the farmers to help India gain independence from price rise as the government worked out a whopping 7,350 per cent increase in pulses procurement at MSP.[24] Price rise of pulses became history.

Total fertilizer subsidy increased by 500 per cent in 2022–23[25] from 2021–22, while a total of 23 crore Soil Health Cards were distributed. As many as 1,260 *mandis* (large markets) were linked through eNAM. The impact was seen in the rising exports of agricultural produces. Non-basmati rice exports rose by 110 per cent. The Modi government extended ₹4.7 lakh crore credit to 4 crore farmers through Kisan Credit Cards.[26] Besides, ₹1.32 lakh crore was settled in claim under the Pradhan Mantri Fasal Bima Yojana.[27]

The Modi government stood by farmers with support across various stages of the agriculture cycle – seeds to soil health, insurance to irrigation, MSP to markets. This was in line with the comprehensive approach to empower farmers at every step. For market linkages to improve farmers' income, eNAM, the unified national market, increased competition while providing better price discovery for the farmers in a transparent manner. At the same time, the thrust of the Modi government on Farmer Producer Organisations (FPOs) helped in the realization of better prices and higher returns for farmers.

Mega food parks also gained in strength, from just two in 2014 to twenty-three in March 2023.[28]

Start-up ecosystem in agriculture also found a firm foothold as 1,138 start-ups in agriculture and allied sectors from 2019–20 to 2022–23 were sanctioned ₹70.30 crores of grant-in-aid.[29]

Women First

Prime Minister Narendra Modi has accorded the highest importance to Matri Shakti. Women-led growth is India's story for the world community. Paid maternity leaves were hiked from twelve weeks to twenty-six weeks by the Modi government, while over 3.3 crore women were paid ₹6,000 each under Pradhan Mantri Matru Vandana Yojana. Besides, a permanent commission for women in armed forces was instituted. All wings of the Army now see women's participation. Under the watch of PM Modi, over 27 crore MUDRA loans to women beneficiaries were sanctioned as a true commitment to enlist Matri Shakti in the development path of the country.[30]

The Modi government also took a host of steps to empower women, which included the proposal to raise marriageable age of women from eighteen to twenty-one years to boost their prospects for education and employment. The law against Triple Talaq gave freedom to Muslim women from age-old exploitation. An increase in the paid maternity leave period from twelve weeks to twenty-six weeks makes work-life balance possible for working women. Scrapping of Article 35A also gave rights to women in Jammu and Kashmir.

Under Pradhan Mantri Jan Dhan Yojana, the total number of female beneficiaries has been 27.2 crore, while over 27 crore sanitary pads were ensured at ₹1 in Jan Aushadhi Kendras, along with 9.52 lakh toilets built for girls in schools, besides India netting a 100-fold jump in the number of recognized start-ups since 2016.[31]

India – A Start-Up Capital

In a short span of time, under the guiding and nursing care of the Modi government, India became home to more than 100 unicorns, i.e., start-ups valued at more than $1 billion. India also became home to more than 80,000 start-ups. The impact has been seen in the 23 lakh direct and indirect jobs generated through tech start-ups in 2017–21. The total number of recognized Indian start-ups stands at 84,012, out of which India became home to 115 unicorns. There has been a nineteen-fold increase in new start-ups. Number of unicorns increased from 4 in 2014 to 115 in 2023.[32]

One of the greatest examples of improvement in the business climate of the country can be seen among start-ups. Before 2014, India had around 350 start-ups. In the nine years of the Modi government, the nurture through Start-Up India and Stand Up India helped a 260-fold increase in the number of start-ups.

Friendly Taxation

The number of IT returns has increased from 3.35 crore in FY 2013–14 to 6.85 crore in FY 2022–23.[33] Taxation in India is now people-friendly. The days of tax terrorism are now history. E-filing of tax returns has now become the norm and refunds are credited into bank accounts within a few days. At the same time, faceless assessments and appeals reduce harassment of the assessees. Tax rates have actually reduced with the government ensuring that taxation is not stingy but a contribution of the people in the exercise of nation-building. In the true spirit of a trusted and trusting government, an atmosphere of mutual trust has been created by taking steps like enabling self-attestation. Also, the government has shown it trusts citizens. This helped in the increase in the number of IT returns.

Care for People

Caring for the people has been the key mantra of the Modi government. The dream of owning a house was within everyone's reach, whether poor or middle class. For the poor, there is Pradhan Mantri Awas Yojana in both rural and urban areas. The Credit Linked Subsidy scheme (CLSS) for middle-income group brought down interest rates on housing loans substantially, helping more than 6 lakh middle-class buyers to purchase their first home. At the same time, institutional and legislative reforms in the form of the unveiling of the Real Estate (Regulation and Development) Act (RERA) ensured timely delivery of homes to the buyers who were stuck in unfinished projects because of the impunity enjoyed by the builders during the Congress-led government at the Centre. It was ensured that the money of homebuyers was not stuck endlessly.

The mobility of the people, essential for the middle class and the people at large, was also attended to by boosting ease of travel with improved connectivity. Expansion of metro rail made mobility in cities easier for urban residents. Also, the *Ude Desh ka Aam Naagrik* (UDAN) scheme unveiled affordable air travel and connectivity to many tier-2 and tier-3 cities.

It is worthwhile to note that metro connectivity increased from five cities in 2014 to twenty in 2023. Besides, 2,435 electric buses are deployed across the country as part of the drive for green mobility and also in affirmation of India's commitment to sustainable development goals.[34]

The people also found the caring touch of the Modi government in the form of the cost of internet data coming down by 95 per cent.[35] Besides, 2.86 crore electricity connections, 9.6 crore LPG connections and 49.03 crore bank accounts[36] were activated as part of the commitment of the Modi government to bring tangible changes in the lives of the people.

3

Narendra Modi Delivers Solution-based G20

Prime Minister Narendra Modi chairing a discussion at the G20 Summit in New Delhi

Prime Minister Narendra Modi's global leadership saw the Indian G20 presidency deliver the most comprehensive action plan to meet the challenges posed by a host of issues faced by humanity. For the first time, the developed countries committed to fulfilling their commitments of $100 billion in financing climate action projects in developing countries in 2023 on the urging of Modi.

The G20 joint statement Delhi Declaration ran into eighty-three paragraphs,[1] addressing each issue haunting global humanity, from the Russia–Ukraine conflict to shortages of food and fertilizer, from regulating crypto currency to addressing growing debts of poor nations, from climate mitigation to bridging digital divide, from ensuring equity in health and education to women-led development, from committing to the timeline of meeting the targets of sustainable development goals to bridging the gap between the Global North and Global South.

'At the place where we are gathered today, just a few kilometers away from here, stands a pillar that is nearly two and a half thousand years old. Inscribed on this pillar in the Prakrit language are the words: "हेवम लोकसा हितमुखे ति, अथ इयम नातिसु हेवम," meaning, "The welfare and happiness of humanity should always be ensured." Two and a half thousand years ago, the land of India gave this message to the entire world,' said Modi at the inauguration of the G20 Leaders' Summit to set the tone for solution-based outcomes for the multilateral meeting.

The prime minister rightly said that after COVID-19, a huge crisis of lack of trust has come in the world. 'Conflict has deepened this trust deficit. Just as we can overcome COVID, we can also overcome this crisis of mutual trust. Today, as the president of the G20, India invites the entire world to come together and, first and foremost, transform this Global Trust Deficit into global trust and confidence,' Modi said in his initial remarks at the inauguration of the summit. 'This is a time for all of us to walk together, and the mantra of "*sabka saath, sabka vikas; sabka vishwas and sabka prayas*" can become a guiding light for all of us.' Modi's words were aimed at healing the wounds of global humanity. He said,

> Whether it is a turbulent global economy or the North–South divide, or the distance between East and West, Management of Food, Fuel, and Fertilizer, or dealing with Terrorism and Cybersecurity, or ensuring Health, Energy and Water Security, we must move towards concrete solutions for these challenges, not just for the present but also for future generations.

Modi rightly asserted that India's G20 presidency became a symbol of inclusion both within the country and beyond, representing the spirit of *sabka saath*. It has become the people's G20, he said:

> Millions of Indians have engaged with it. Over 200 meetings have been held in more than 60 cities across the country. It was in the spirit of *sabka saath* that India proposed permanent membership for the African Union in the G20.

Modi made the exhortation that the '21st century is a time that has the potential to give new direction to the entire world. It's a time when years old challenges demand new solutions from us. Therefore, we must move forward by fulfilling all our responsibilities with a human-centric approach', the heads of the states were nodding in agreement with visible appreciation for the leadership of Modi and Bharat.

The preamble of the joint statement thus began:

> We are 'One Earth, One Family', and we share One Future. We, the Leaders of the G20, met in New Delhi on 9–10 September 2023, under the theme 'Vasudhaiva

> Kutumbakam'. We meet at a defining moment in history where the decisions we make now will determine the future of our people and our planet. It is with the philosophy of living in harmony with our surrounding ecosystem that we commit to concrete actions to address global challenges. (Delhi Declaration)

The next few paragraphs of the Delhi Declaration set the tone for the global agenda for action as well as a template for the world to live in peace:

> G20 cooperation is essential in determining the course the world takes. Headwinds to global economic growth and stability persist. Years of cascading challenges and crises have reversed gains in the 2030 Agenda and its Sustainable Development Goals (SDGs). Global greenhouse gas (GHG) emissions continue to increase, with climate change, biodiversity loss, pollution, drought, land degradation and desertification threatening lives and livelihoods. Rising commodity prices, including food and energy prices, are contributing to cost-of-living pressures. Global challenges like poverty and inequality, climate change, pandemics and conflicts disproportionately affect women and children, who are the most vulnerable.
>
> Together we have an opportunity to build a better future. Just energy transitions can improve jobs and livelihoods, and strengthen economic resilience. We affirm that no country should have to choose between fighting poverty and fighting for our planet. We will pursue development models that implement sustainable, inclusive and just transitions globally, while leaving no one behind.

As Leaders of G20, the premier global forum for international economic cooperation, we resolve to act in concrete ways through partnerships.

We commit to:

a. Accelerate strong, sustainable, balanced and inclusive growth.

b. Accelerate the full and effective implementation of the 2030 Agenda for Sustainable Development.

c. Pursue low-GHG/low-carbon emissions, climate-resilient and environmentally sustainable development pathways by championing an integrated and inclusive approach. We will urgently accelerate our actions to address development and climate challenges, promote Lifestyles for Sustainable Development (LiFE), and conserve biodiversity, forests and oceans.

d. Improve access to medical countermeasures and facilitate more supplies and production capacities in developing countries to prepare better for future health emergencies.

e. Promote resilient growth by urgently and effectively addressing debt vulnerabilities in developing countries.

f. Scale up financing from all sources for accelerating progress on SDGs.

g. Accelerate efforts and enhance resources towards achieving the Paris Agreement including its temperature goal.

h. Pursue reforms for better, bigger and more effective Multilateral Development Banks (MDBs) to address global challenges to maximize developmental impact.

i. Improve access to digital services and digital public infrastructure, and leverage digital transformation opportunities to boost sustainable and inclusive growth.

j. Promote sustainable, quality, healthy, safe and gainful employment.

k. Close gender gaps and promote the full, equal, effective and meaningful participation of women in the economy as decision-makers.

l. Better integrate the perspectives of developing countries including LDCs, LLDCs and SIDS, into future G20 agenda and strengthen the voice of developing countries in global decision-making.

Through these actions today, we are building towards a system that better empowers countries to address global challenges, is human-centric, and brings prosperity and well-being to humanity. For the Planet, People, Peace and Prosperity.

We note with deep concern the immense human suffering and the adverse impact of wars and conflicts around the world.

Concerning the war in Ukraine, while recalling the discussion in Bali, we reiterated our national positions and resolutions adopted at the UN Security Council and the UN General Assembly (A/RES/ES-11/1 and A/RES/ES-11/6) and underscored that all states must act in a manner consistent with the Purposes and Principles of the UN Charter in its entirety. In line with the UN Charter, all states must refrain from the threat or use of force to seek territorial acquisition against the territorial integrity and sovereignty or political independence of any state. The use or threat of use of nuclear weapons is inadmissible.

Reaffirming that the G20 is the premier forum for international economic cooperation, and recognizing that while the G20 is not the platform to resolve geopolitical and security issues, we acknowledge that these issues can have significant consequences for the global economy.

We highlighted the human suffering and negative added impacts of the war in Ukraine with regard to global food and energy security, supply chains, macro-financial stability, inflation and growth, which has complicated the policy environment for countries, especially developing and least developed countries, which are still recovering from the COVID-19 pandemic and the economic disruption which has derailed progress towards the SDGs. There were different views and assessments of the situation.

We appreciate the efforts of Türkiye and UN-brokered Istanbul Agreements consisting of the Memorandum of Understanding between the Russian Federation and the Secretariat of the United Nations on Promoting Russian Food Products and Fertilizers to the World Markets and the Initiative on the Safe Transportation of Grain and Foodstuffs from Ukrainian Ports (Black Sea Initiative), and call for their full, timely and effective implementation to ensure the immediate and unimpeded deliveries of grain, foodstuffs and fertilizers/inputs from the Russian Federation and Ukraine. This is necessary to meet the demand in developing and least developed countries, particularly those in Africa.

In this context, emphasizing the importance of sustaining food and energy security, we called for the cessation of military destruction or other attacks on relevant infrastructure. We also expressed deep concern about the adverse impact that conflicts have on the security of civilians, thereby exacerbating existing socio-economic fragilities and vulnerabilities and hindering an effective humanitarian response.

> We call on all states to uphold the principles of international law including territorial integrity and sovereignty, international humanitarian law, and the multilateral system that safeguards peace and stability. The peaceful resolution of conflicts, and efforts to address crises as well as diplomacy and dialogue are critical. We will unite in our endeavour to address the adverse impact of the war on the global economy and welcome all relevant and constructive initiatives that support a comprehensive, just and durable peace in Ukraine that will uphold all the Purposes and Principles of the UN Charter for the promotion of peaceful, friendly, and good neighbourly relations among nations in the spirit of 'One Earth, One Family, One Future'.
>
> Today's era must not be of war. A Strong, Sustainable, Balanced and Inclusive Growth Global Economic Situation
>
> Cascading crises have posed challenges to long-term growth. Facing an uneven recovery, and cognizant of the need to boost long-term growth, we will implement well-calibrated macroeconomic and structural policies. We will protect the vulnerable, through promoting equitable growth and enhancing macroeconomic and financial stability. Such an approach will help resolve the cost-of-living crisis and unlock strong, sustainable, balanced, and inclusive growth.

The G20 presidency led to many new initiatives and achievements. India took the lead in the annual G20 foreign ministers' meeting by being the first to deliver a fully negotiated and embraced G20 chair's summary and outcome document.

This comprehensive document highlighted critical themes relevant to member states including the strengthening of multilateralism, countering terrorism and addressing global health concerns, among others.

'It is India's presidency that played host to the inaugural "Voice of the Global South Summit". With participation from 125 countries across 10 sessions spanning 2 days, this landmark event provided a platform for participants to voice the concerns, ideas, challenges, and priorities of the developing world,' said a senior functionary.

The G20 Meeting of Agricultural Chief Scientists (MACS) during India's presidency supported the launch of Millets and other Ancient Grains International Research Initiative (MAHARISHI), which is an endeavour to establish mechanisms to connect researchers and institutions, encourage information sharing and organize capacity-building activities, among others, across the G20 countries.

The inception meeting of the G20 EMPOWER group was held under India's presidency. G20 Alliance for the Empowerment and Progression of Women's Economic Representation (EMPOWER) is an alliance of G20 business leaders and governments that aims to accelerate women's leadership and empowerment in the private sector.

After the G20 Digital Economy Ministers' Meeting, a consensus was reached on creating the Digital Public Infrastructures (DPIs). Also, consensus was built around 'Cyber Security in the Digital Economy' and Digital Skills.

During India's G20 presidency, the meeting of G20 Chief Science Advisers Roundtable (G20-CSAR) was also initiated, which deliberated on issues like opportunities in 'One Health' for better disease control and pandemic preparedness; synergizing global efforts to expand access to scholarly scientific knowledge; diversity, equity, inclusion and accessibility in science and technology; and an institutional mechanism for inclusive, continuous and action-oriented global S&T policy dialogue.

In an endeavour to reform and reinforce multilateralism, India also revitalized discussions surrounding reforms of international institutions including UN Security Council and multilateral development banks (MDBs). It was during India's presidency that an Independent Expert Group was established to provide recommendations for bolstering MDBs and improving their efficiency in confronting 21st-century challenges.

Indian G20 Sherpa Amitabh Kant rightly said that the Delhi Declaration was the most comprehensive document ever delivered by the multilateral group, and the credit went to Modi for bringing all the member nations on board for a shared vision to deal with the global challenges. The icing on the cake, again on the initiative of Modi, was the induction of the African Union in G20, which was the most definitive step to bridge the gap between the Global South and Global North, as well as to provide a credible platform to the African nations to raise their voices. The world media rightly hailed Modi for wrapping up the induction of the African Union into the G20 in record time, with the application submitted in June 2023 and becoming a member of the group in September, all in just three months. This is a defining statement of the Modi path to scale up and deliver on the vision for a shared destiny of the global community with a clear approach that no one should be left behind.

4

The Modi Doctrine for Global Good

Prime Minister Narendra Modi leads G20 leaders to pay floral tributes to Mahatma Gandhi at Raj Ghat, New Delhi

Prime Minister Narendra Modi has caused a tectonic shift in India's bilateral relations with the US. His summit with the US president Joe Biden had the global community glued to television screens as they witnessed history unfolding in Washington, DC. The two heads of state discussed ways to work together for the global community. They firmed up their resolves to work as equal partners to shape the course of the century.

PM Modi also presented democracy as solution for a host of global challenges. Democracy runs in the veins of India, said PM Modi during a press conference with President Biden. Dialogue is the lifeline of democracy. PM Modi, by underlining that dialogue, not war, is the way out of conflicts in his speech to the US Congress, once more allowed American Congressmen and senators to witness an exceptional statesman in their midst.

There emerged a consensus among the Republicans and Democrats that PM Modi wasn't just speaking for India or for the benefits of his country; he was giving voice to the cause of the global community. They once more understood the significance of the Indian philosophy of 'Vasudhev Kutumbkam' – the world is one family – and that in the common good lies the well-being of all.

Democracy delivers, said PM Modi. He asserted that the thriving Indian democracy breathes in over 250 political parties in India with twenty of them ruling in several states. Such diversity is not to be found elsewhere. The Americans sought endorsement for their own diversity by bonding with India. They also found, to their great satisfaction, that PM Modi is a champion of human values. 'Indian democracy functions on the Constitution, and the statute book provides for access to all the programmes and schemes run by the government without discrimination on the basis of caste, creed, religion, age and regions. This is stated in the mantra of *sabka vikas, sabka vishwas, sabka prayas*,' said PM Modi, as he spoke of the inclusive nature of the Indian democracy during the joint press conference with President Biden.[1]

The leadership of the US accorded PM Modi a place of eminence with an unprecedented reception for him at the White House. The Indian diaspora made a strong presence in the backyard of the White House to witness the unfolding of history. During the tech summit attended by PM Modi and President Biden, a number of CEOs of the well-known American corporate giants were people of Indian origin. The 3.5 million strong Indian diaspora in the US have been the brand ambassadors of India. They are the vital organs of the American economy. This was evident during the visit of PM Modi to the US and was richly acknowledged by the Biden administration.

'When I came here last, India was the tenth largest economy of the world. Now, India is the fifth largest economy of the world. Soon, India will be the third largest economy of the world,' PM Modi told the US Congress. The US, the largest economy in the world, laid the red carpet for the Prime Minister of India, who is scripting rapid economic growth for his country with eyes set on the target of becoming the third largest economy in the world. This is significant because India and the US bilateral trade has crossed $190 billion, which was also stressed by President Biden.

This set up the vast scope of collaborations unveiled during PM Modi's visit to the US. From the Artemis agreement for cooperation between the National Aeronautics and Space Administration (NASA) and the Indian Space Research Organisation (ISRO), the deal for the production of jet engines by General Electric in India and setting up a manufacturing plant for semiconductors in Gujarat, besides India procuring the predator drones, revealed the beginning of an era of strategic cooperation between the two democracies working for the global good.

The Modi doctrine calls for a strong India, which is being fulfilled through the Atmanirbhar Bharat campaign. In the defence sector, the collaboration between the US and India promises to accelerate self-reliance in the production of defence goods. Not only gaining self-reliance, but India must also be armed with weapons, assets and technology to gain an edge. This again is in the interest of global good because India is looked upon by several nations in the immediate neighbourhood of South Asia, Indian Ocean, Indo-Pacific and elsewhere as a source of security and strength. This has been affirmed recently by the Indian Coast Guard crackdown against the trafficking of drugs through the sea routes.

India and the US, PM Modi said, are partners also for clean energy transition as the global community looks upon the two countries to fightback climate change. This is befitting the leadership role of India in climate mitigation efforts. India alone has acted decisively on Paris Accord to demonstrate the Modi doctrine for global good in action.

Prime Minister Narendra Modi has left a lasting imprint on India's foreign policy and engagement with the world. At the core of the Modi touch to India's foreign policy is care for global humanity in the true spirit of 'Vasudhev Kutumbakam'. This has been reflected in India's persistent efforts towards making a strong contribution to international peace, stability, growth and security at every multilateral forum. For this, India drew global attention to the most pressing challenges faced by humanity including through Mission LiFE, aimed at democratizing climate action and empowering people to adopt climate-friendly lifestyles and the popularization of millets to address the challenge of food security.

India stands for an inclusive human-centric approach to development while seeking the use of technology to transform lives of people globally. For this purpose, India is making determined efforts for reformed multilateralism so as to ensure a more accountable, inclusive and representative international system.

India is actively engaging in various multilateral forums like the United Nations (UN), G20, Shanghai Cooperation Organization (SCO), BRICS, the International Solar Alliance, the Coalition for Disaster Resilient Infrastructure, etc. PM Modi's emphasis during India's G20 presidency was seen in the theme 'One Earth, One Family, One Future'. This enshrines advocacy for inclusive and resilient growth. PM Modi's concern for the well-being of global humanity has also been seen during the G20 push for progress on Sustainable Development Goals, while clear thrust was given to green development and Mission LiFE. At the same time, the thrust during the Indian G20 presidency on technological transformation and public digital infrastructure was truly for equity in progress for global humanity. This again saw PM Modi bring the core philosophy of his governance to care for the last man in queue in his world vision.

Truly, PM Modi stands tall in seeking accountability from global multilateral agencies, which calls for reforming multilateral institutions. India also seeks women-led development, besides international peace and harmony. Those following the Modi model of development would clearly relate to the efforts to put women at the forefront of developmental works within the country as seen through the Pradhan Mantri Awas Yojna and other programmes.

The most decisive and formidable imprint of PM Modi in India's foreign affairs has been the country taking on the leadership role of the Global South by amplifying the voice and concerns of the developing countries. At the G20 Development Ministers Meeting held in Varanasi on 12 June 2023,[2] the G20 Development Ministers endorsed the work done by the Development Working Group and unanimously adopted two outcome documents: G20 2023 Action Plan on Accelerating Progress on the SDGs and High-level Principles on Lifestyles for Sustainable Development.

India under the leadership of PM Modi has seen higher standing and greater influence in various international institutions and multilateral forums, and in the larger footprint of Indians in every walk of life across the globe, contributing to stronger global common good. There is global recognition today that India is a force of global good in the world. India is reckoned as a force for regional and global stability, peace and prosperity.

Under the leadership of PM Modi, India was elected as a non-permanent member of the United Nations Security Council (UNSC) for the eighth time for the 2021–22 term with an overwhelming majority (184 of 193 votes) during the elections held in June 2020 in New York.[3]

In August 2021, PM Modi chaired an open debate of the UNSC on international maritime security. It was for the first time in seventy-five years that the prime minister of India chaired a meeting of the UNSC on the issue of maritime security. During another signature event at the UNSC on technology and peacekeeping, a first of its kind UNSC resolution on 'protecting the protectors' with a focus on accountability for crimes against UN peacekeepers as well as a presidential statement on technology and peacekeeping were unanimously adopted. As a leading troop-contributing country to UN peacekeeping missions, the use of technology in UN peacekeeping is an important focus for India.

India donated $1.6 million to the UN to develop a situational awareness platform called Unite Aware for the benefit of peacekeeping missions. This software platform aims to provide real-time, updated data on a range of parameters, such as topography, demography, security situation, etc., to peacekeepers deployed in conflict areas.

During this tenure as a non-permanent member, India also served as the chair of the 1988 (Taliban) sanctions committee and 1970 (Libya) sanctions committee of the UNSC for two years and of the 1373 (counter terrorism) committee for the year 2022. During India's second presidency of the UNSC in December 2022, a high-level open debate was organized on the theme of new orientation for reformed multilateralism. The primary focus of the open debate was on reforming multilateralism and encouraging all member states to decisively address the pressing needs for such reforms in the global governance architecture including the long-debated reforms in the UNSC.

For the first time, India brought up the UNSC reform debate. As the chair of the important Counter Terrorism Committee (CTC) of the UNSC in 2022, a historic and successful special meeting of the CTC was held for two days in Mumbai and Delhi in October 2022. This was the first time the UNSC convened in India in any format. Again, for the first time, all fifteen members of the UNSC jointly paid tribute to the victims of terrorism at the 26/11 memorial at Taj Palace Hotel in Mumbai on 28 October 2022.

The special meeting of the CTC in Delhi on 29 October 2022 unanimously adopted the 'Delhi Declaration' on 'Countering the Use of New and Emerging Technologies for Terrorist Purposes'. In December 2022, during our second presidency of the UNSC, the external affairs minister chaired a high-level UNSC briefing on 'Global Counter Terrorism Approach: Challenges and Way Forward'. Following this briefing, the UNSC approved a security council presidential statement on counter terrorism. India also held the third 'No Money for Terror' ministerial conference to strengthen global efforts against terrorism. India co-sponsored a landmark UNGA resolution (A/RES/76/268) on multilingualism, which was unanimously adopted on 10 June 2022. For the first time, this resolution mentioned the Hindi language, encouraging the UN Department of Global Communications to continue disseminating important communications and messages in official as well as non-official languages, including Hindi.

On 21 June 2023, PM Modi led the Yoga Day celebrations at the UN headquarters, creating the Guinness World Record for the participation of people of most nationalities in a single yoga session. The idea for declaring an International Day of Yoga (IDY) at the United Nations was formally proposed by the prime minister in his maiden address to the 69th UNGA on 27 September 2014.

The resolution establishing the IDY was co-sponsored by 177 countries and adopted by the UNGA in December 2014. 'Mission LIFE' was launched by the prime minister in 2022. The UN secretary general travelled to India to grace the occasion. At the launch, leaders from across the world joined PM Modi by sending video messages supporting the Mission LiFE initiative. India successfully sponsored a UNGA resolution, declaring the year 2023 as the 'International Year of Millets'.

The resolution, supported by more than seventy countries, is intended to increase public awareness on the health benefits of millets and their suitability for cultivation under tough conditions marked by climate change.

To ensure that the G20 presidency focused on the priorities, perspectives and concerns of the developing world, India organized the first-ever 'Voice of Global South Summit' in January 2023. High-level participation from 125 countries reflected their trust in India's efforts towards building a prosperous and inclusive future for the entire world.

India engages as a member of Missile Technology Control Regime (MTCR), Wassenaar Arrangement (WA) and Australia Group (AG). India assumed the plenary chairmanship of WA from 1 January 2023 for a period of one year, which is significant considering that India became the latest member of WA only around five years back, in December 2017.

India joined the Shanghai Cooperation Organisation (SCO) as a full member state in the year 2017 and held the first-ever presidency of SCO from 17 September 2022 to 4 July 2023. In this period, India hosted around 134 events including 14 ministerial-level meetings with a key focus on SECURE: security, economic development, connectivity, unity, respect for sovereignty and territorial integrity and environmental protection. India also successfully created five new pillars of cooperation in SCO, namely start-ups and innovations, traditional medicine, digital inclusion, youth empowerment and shared Buddhist heritage. India hosted the heads of state summit of the SCO on 4 July 2023 in a virtual format.

India's leadership of the organization has led to various meaningful outcome documents such as the 'New Delhi Declaration' and two other statements of the heads of state on 'Countering Radicalization Leading to Terrorism, Separatism and Extremism and on Cooperation in Digital Transformation'. India also successfully introduced the concept of de-carbonization of transport, promotion of digital transformation and innovative technologies to achieve higher efficiency and sustainability, which was endorsed by heads of all member states of the SCO.

At India's initiative, two new mechanisms (working groups) were created: Special Working Group on Startups and Innovation and an Experts Working Group on Traditional Medicine.

International Society of Automation (ISA) aims to provide collective work towards the massive deployment of solar energy in terms of technology, finance and capacity building.

As of July 2023, the ISA has strengthened its membership with 116 countries, which includes 94 member countries (countries having ratified the ISA framework agreement) and 22 signatory countries (countries having signed but yet to ratify the ISA framework agreement).

India through its dedicated initiative of Coalition for Disaster Resilient Infrastructure (CDRI) is bringing together nations to build a future that is disaster resilient through disaster- and climate-resilient infrastructure. India prioritizes localizing disaster and climate resilience information and technical capacity building through CDRI.

5

India: A Global Anchor

Prime Minister Narendra Modi at the launch of the deposit insurance scheme in New Delhi

India quickly evacuated over 3,500 citizens from Sudan.[1] Prime Minister Narendra Modi called an emergency meeting soon after violence broke out in Sudan. He sent out a clear message that each minute is crucial for the safe evacuation of the Indian citizens.

Operation Kaveri was set in motion with INS *Sumedha* and INS *Tarkash* quickly sailing the international waters, while the Indian Air Force pressed in the service heavy transport carriers such as C-130J, C-17, etc. India activated its logistics and diplomatic assets in Saudi Arabia, and Jeddah became a point of contact for the evacuated Indians for their onward journey back home.

Except for one unfortunate death of an Indian, Albert Augestine, in Sudan, the joint efforts of the Indian Air Force and the Indian Navy in close collaboration with the diplomatic corps have once more demonstrated that India has come a long way in becoming the first responder in crisis for her own people and others as well. This has been made possible because of decisive leadership, which doesn't lose time and stays ahead in anticipating the turn of events in regions of strife.

Also, 'Operation Sankat Mochan', carried out in 2016 in South Sudan, remained a torchlight for the Indian rescue mission once more in the African nation. 'Operation Samudra Sethu' in 2020 had also brought 3,992 Indians back home during the COVID-19 pandemic.[2] By now, it has been well demonstrated that Indians will not be the last but the first to be rescued, and the world has noted the growing strength of the Indian passport.

True to the Indian philosophy that the world is one family, the Indian evacuation efforts didn't differentiate between nationalities. This was acknowledged by the president of France Emmanuel Macron who thanked PM Modi for rescuing and evacuating the French embassy staffers from Khartoum, the Sudanese capital.

Sudan crisis reminded the global community of India's capabilities in evacuating the people stuck in the strife-torn regions. Only recently, India carried out one of the largest rescue and evacuation missions 'Operation Ganga' in Ukraine. Thousands of Indian students stuck in

Ukraine were evacuated safely from the conflict-ridden region in circumstances that tested the depth of India's diplomatic ties with Eastern European nations and also the manoeuvrability of the logistics.

The ministers camped in the capitals of nations bordering Ukraine, while PM Modi worked with Russian and Ukrainian leadership to even pause aggression for limited hours to allow the Indian students to cross over to safe zones. Along with the Indian students, India was able to evacuate and rescue scores of people of other countries. India made it clear that there is no discrimination or distinction in service to humanity. The global community was in full praise of the scale of the operation carried out by India in Ukraine. This again has been singularly made possible because of the political capital deployed in responding to humanitarian crisis in any part of the world.

In 2015, India had carried out a large-scale evacuation exercise from Yemen as part of 'Operation Raahat', evacuating 6,710 individuals – 4,748 Indians and 1,962 foreign nationals.[3] Indian rescue missions have now become household names with films and web series made about them, something which earlier used to be seen only in American films.

Incidentally, Union Minister for External Affairs S. Jaishankar has been on record recalling PM Modi's personal involvement in addressing the crisis in any part of the world. Jaishankar was pleasantly surprised when he saw PM Modi ringing him on his mobile phone late after midnight to enquire about the rescue efforts after the Indian embassy in Kabul had been attacked by terrorists.

'Operation Devi Shakti' evacuated Indian citizens and foreign nationals from Afghanistan after the Taliban captured power in Kabul.

India is now being globally acknowledged as a country with impeccable capabilities to respond in situations of natural disaster. Within hours of the earthquakes jolting Turkey, PM Modi had already held an emergency meeting and the special teams of the National Disaster Response Force (NDRF) were airborne to respond to one of the gravest tragedies in the last few decades. The team of doctors, paramedics and other NDRF personnel who carried out relief work as part of 'Operation Dost' won the hearts of the people in Turkey with their quick response to save lives. The Indian efforts in Turkey have been rightly applauded globally for expeditious response to save lives even in situations which were too harsh in the aftermath of the earthquakes.

Such expertise of India was also seen in the wake of the Nepal earthquakes in 2015 which had left a trail of deaths. The Indian response with 'Operation Maitri' was quick and timely to save precious lives. India in fact has tested its capabilities as the first responder in times of natural disasters as seen during the Bhuj Earthquake and the Uttarakhand floods. The scale has come with a massive investment of the political capital by PM Modi.

India has been the voice of peace since recorded human history. The teachings of peace by Lord Buddha bind India and Japan in deep cultural relations. This was displayed during the G7 summit when Prime Minister Narendra Modi called for diplomacy to resolve conflicts.

'Enmity does not calm enmity. Enmity is pacified by affinity. It is in this spirit, we should move forward together with everyone,' PM Modi referred to the teachings of Lord Buddha while speaking at the ninth working session of the G7 summit. The backdrop was set by the meeting of PM Modi with Ukraine's president Volodymyr Zelenskyy. PM Modi asserted that the current situation went beyond the economy and politics and concerned humanity as a whole.

PM Modi last year in his bilateral meeting with Russian president Vladimir Putin had very unequivocally said that 'today is not the era of war and conflicts must be resolved through dialogue and diplomacy'. Such clarity of expression has rarely been seen among world leaders. Truly, India has become the first responder to any kind of humanitarian crisis in any part of the world. This shows PM Modi speaking always in the interest of humanity.

Indian voice is heard with gravity in the big league of nations as PM Modi brings much weight to his interactions with the global leaders in which he speaks for humanity as a whole and his concerns express the yearnings of all the countries, particularly the developing and the poor countries.

It was against this backdrop that G7 in 2023 listed in its agenda the need to build partnerships with the Global South, a term made popular by India to describe the developing nations, which are facing distinct challenges.

PM Modi in another working group meeting of G7 said:

> Global peace, stability and prosperity are our common objectives. In today's interconnected world, crises in any

> one region affect all the countries. And, the developing countries, which have limited resources, are the worst affected. In the current global situation, these countries are facing the maximum and most profound impact of the food, fuel, and fertilizer crisis.

This again demonstrated PM Modi's firm articulation of the challenges faced by the Global South on issues such as sovereign debt, climate change, food shortages, fertilizer crisis, etc. Yet, he told the leaders of G7 that the world continues to remain stuck in challenges because multilateral agencies, such as the United Nations (UN), are not able to prevent conflicts. PM Modi reminded that the UN was established with the very purpose of establishing peace.

Dissecting the weaknesses of the UN, which badly needs reforms to represent the 21st century, PM Modi firmly stressed that even the definition of terrorism has not been accepted in the UN. His call for introspection and forceful argument for reforms in big institutions like the UN was received well by the G7 leaders.

India for years has been calling for reforms in the UN, and PM Modi reiterated that the multilateral body must also give space to the voice of the Global South. India being a true functional democracy with deep roots has always raised the democratic aspirations of the people. That the UN permanent members owe their positions to the wars of the last century, and countries such as India despite being projected to have the largest population in the world are not in the coveted club, is truly undemocratic.

India has always raised the voice for an international order based on respect for national sovereignty and territorial integrity, underlining the significance of the UN Charter and international law, which was asserted by PM Modi in his speech in the working group meeting of G7.

PM Modi has been regularly attending G7 summits. This acknowledges India's growing image on the world stage. India is now the world's fifth largest economy. Indian economy is bigger than even the four members of G7. Also, India has emerged as the voice of the Global South with the G20 presidency. India will also host the Quad summit in 2024. With PM Modi in the lead, India is now a partner for countries seeking solutions to challenges faced by them.

India, under the leadership of PM Modi, has become a strong voice of the growing debt challenges of developing and poor countries. On climate change also, India is the voice of affected nations. India has forcefully called for the advanced countries to share resources for mitigation efforts including transfer of technology for clean energy, which was again reiterated forcefully by PM Modi before the G7 leaders.

While the G7 summit brainstormed global issues, health ministers of G7 along with outreach countries – India, Indonesia and Thailand – and multilateral agencies brainstormed over global issues in Tokyo, Japan. The G7, a group of the most industrialized nations, has most of the global wealth, and it has a duty to take the lead in addressing the global challenges.

India has been at the centre stage of the deliberations of G7 as Prime Minister Narendra Modi has regularly attended the deliberations as special invitee in line with the recognition of Indian power. India, with the presidency of G20, is currently at the centre stage of solution-based actionable agenda. The success of G7 agenda cannot be achieved unless aligned with the aims and objectives cogently brought forth by India during the G20 presidency.

The world is still learning its way out of the COVID-19 pandemic. The once-in-a-century pandemic has made humanity aware of the health risks of an interconnected world. The outbreak of communicable diseases poses serious challenge to the well-being of the global population. Also, health issues are directly connected with the global economy. Indian G20 presidency, by lending its voice to the Global South, has brought forth the concerns of developing and poor countries about deepening debt, which became acute in the aftermath of the COVID-19 pandemic. It's in this context that the agendas of G7 and G20 must be aligned.

The G7 must take lessons from the Indian way of dealing with the COVID-19 pandemic as it can lead the wealthiest nations to contribute constructively by learning from the leadership of PM Modi. The Indian COVID-19 response was based on the principle that none should be left behind in the vaccination drive. All must be vaccinated, and India demonstrated that people living even in the remotest parts of the country were also provided access to the vaccines.

Malana is one of the villages in Himachal Pradesh. Tradition claims that the descendants of Alexander's army had settled in this remote village. The villagers are particular about protecting their unique culture, and they maintain a distance from others. It was a tough task for the health personnel to vaccinate the people of the village. But PM Modi during his several video conferences with the heads of the districts' administrations had made it clear that none should be left behind in the vaccination drive. The district administration launched a special campaign to convince the people of the village to take the COVID-19 vaccines. There were several far-flung villages in the country which were covered under the vaccination drive. The administrations even used drones. The frontline workers went to even those villages where only one or very few people lived.

India also lived by its philosophy of Vasudhev Kutumbkam, that the world is one family, and provided indigenous vaccines to countries in all parts of the world, from Brazil to Caribbean nations, from Africa to South Asia. This has to be the guiding principle for G7 when the summit addresses the issue of equitable access to vaccines against global communicable diseases.

Under the leadership of PM Modi, India has also shown an inclusive architecture for the overall well-being and health care of the people. Ayushman Bharat is worth mentioning here. India issued additional 22 crore Ayushman health cards in 2022 compared to 13.22 crore cards issued in 2021. Also, the government last year gave coverage of over ₹50,277.4 crore under the Ayushman Bharat scheme. Over 26,000 hospitals have come under the coverage of Ayushman Bharat. India also gave wider access to healthcare through *e-Sanjeevani* by which people can access doctors through telemedicine.

In fact, India was the first country in Asia to roll out container-based hospitals to help people access healthcare in remote parts of the country. Critical care has also been provided in hospitals in 602 districts of the country. From 387 medical colleges in the country in 2013–14, India now has 648 medical colleges.[4]

The Modi government's emphasis on health care for all has also been attracting foreign direct investments in record numbers. The FDI in pharmaceutical sector has jumped from ₹3,650 crore in 2019–20 to ₹14,677 crore in 2022–23.[5]

The G7 summit can look at the Indian expertise in vaccine development and manufacturing as well as the knowledge gained during the outbreak of the COVID-19 pandemic to make an actionable plan for the well-being of the global population.

6

Modi and India First

Prime Minister Narendra Modi during his visit to Manipur

Prime Minister Narendra Modi has given India First governance in the last nine years. In each area of governance, India First has been the guiding principle. India's national interests guide its governance. In the last nine years, PM Modi has shown 'Yes, we can do it' approach. This has worked wonders.

India is now the fifth largest economy. Developed world wants India on its side. Developing countries want India to be their voice. The poor nations look at India with hope. The small island nations in the Pacific, Indian Ocean, Caribbean and elsewhere have seen India as their saviour. African and Latin American nations have seen

Indian healing touch when the COVID-19 pandemic wreaked havoc across the globe.

It was PM Modi who went to Australia in 2014, after a gap of twenty-eight years, to deepen the bond between the two nations. Now, India and Australia are strategic partners. There are several countries, including Papua New Guinea, where PM Modi's visits were first in several years. This approach with the 360-degree foreign policy has helped India in gaining several friends and well-wishers all across the globe. Now, Indians in any part of the world are warmly received. The Indian passport has weight at the immigration offices. Indian tricolour is well recognized. This was made possible by PM Modi's India First policy and also by putting into practice the ancient philosophy of 'Vasudhev Kutumbkam'.

PM Modi has also freed the entrepreneurial power of the youth of the country. This he did by pushing India First policy in the sphere of the economy. The GEM portal has eliminated the scope for middlemen. This has helped the businessmen without any bias and hindrance bid for the procurements by the government departments. It brought the much-needed confidence among the businessmen that they can take part in economic activities without paying bribes.

The spread of confidence touched the youngsters. Over one lakh start-ups were founded in recent years. More than 100 are now unicorns, with a valuation exceeding $1 billion. One such start-up from Hyderabad even launched a small satellite. PM Modi's India First policy saw the government opening the space sector for private companies. Now, hundreds of start-ups are working in the space sector by taking advantage of the opening up of this sector.

The India First mantra brought the '*Panch Pran of Amrit Kaal*' – goal of developed India; to remove any trace of colonial mindset; take pride in our roots; unity among all Indians; and sense of duty among citizens.

The five guiding principles were backed by actions, and they are showing results. India improved its ranking in the ease of doing business by moving from 142 in 2014 to 63 in 2019, which now has moved to 43. Several offences under the Companies Act were decriminalized to instil confidence among businessmen.

The India First policy has seen unemployment decline to 6.8 per cent in January 2023 from 7.2 per cent in January 2020.[1] Skill enhancement amongst the youth has gained pace. Bilateral agreements with a few developed countries for skilling of the youth to their requirement has added more momentum. The state governments have also now realized that they must dedicate their resources to the skill enhancement of the youth.

This again is the result of India First policy of PM Modi that India has emerged as the second largest manufacturer of mobile phones. India has also taken huge strides in the automobile sector. India First policy guided in policy thrust to gain self-reliance in the manufacturing of chips. Two big-ticket FDIs have come to Gujarat and Karnataka to help India achieve self-reliance in the manufacturing of chips.

India First policy again was in action when PM Modi launched the Atmanirbhar campaign for the defence sector.

Several weapons, ammunitions, equipment and others, which were imported in the past, have to be compulsorily manufactured within India. This shift has created a vibrant private sector working in the defence area. Also, a number of start-ups have joined the Atmanirbhar campaign. The linkages between the research and development agencies of the government and the private sector as part of the hand-holding exercise have helped in creating competitive firms that are competing with the best in the world.

The India First policy has also been guiding India on the path of expansion of the economy. PM Modi has given special focus on infrastructure. PM Gati Shakti Scheme has become a key intervention.

India is also looking to become top global destination for tourists. With G20 presidency, PM Modi has brought the positive image of India to several countries. Now, people in several countries are curious about India. It is to the credit of the India First policy of PM Modi that policy attention has been given to sectors that were never paid attention to, which are now giving new dimensions to the economy.

Prime Minister Narendra Modi in his address to the World Bank's programme on 'Making It Personal: How Behavioural Change Can Tackle Climate Change' made the forceful arguments to take climate action to the dinner table. This, by all accounts, is the most logical action in the battle against climate change.

Individual ownership of climate change, which affects all without discriminating on income, caste, creed, religion, nationality and class, is the need of the hour. In fact, the International Energy Agency in a report has stated that seventy-five individual actions can help cut down almost 2 billion tonne of carbon emissions by 2030.

Each one of us has equal stake in protecting the climate. The world is now far more aware about the climate changes. The episodes of prolonged drought and super floods, which have been seen across the continents, should leave none in doubt about the immediacy of climate change. This is no more knocking at the doors. Climate change has entered our houses, and the time is now for each one of us to fight the demon with all our might.

India has always played a leading role in protecting environment. The Indian way of life is in sync with the environment. Trees have been worshipped in India for ages. Animals have been part of the Indian culture, and they are venerated. The Indian way of life is incomplete without nature. Thus, PM Modi has very forcefully made the world hear the Indian voice for mitigating climate change with due respect.

Therefore, PM Modi rightly said that we must eliminate food wastage from our dining table. The call is timely, as one-third of food gets wasted annually across the world.[2] Here, Mission LiFE, launched jointly by PM Modi and the UN general secretary in October 2022 is a timely intervention in effecting the necessary behavioural changes to achieve the nationally committed goals to cut down emissions and help the world bring down the rising temperature.

PM Modi's leadership in the Global South, the developing nations, has come to a crucial stage. The developed world must commit to its share of responsibility with adequate funding for climate mitigation efforts in the developing and poor countries. With the Indian G20 presidency, the voices of Global South have gained prominence on critical issues, including climate change.

Union Minister for Environment, Forest and Climate Change Bhupender Yadav has strongly raised the Indian voice in the global forums where he has highlighted that India has taken several actions in the last few years to demonstrate the actionable agenda for the world. For instance, India has acted with speed in the mass adoption of LED lights to save energy. India has already distributed 37 crore LED bulbs to the people, which will help in cutting down 3.9 billion tonne of carbon emissions. India has been making intense efforts in energy conservation as the effects of the combined efforts will be seen in saving of 22 billion power units.[3]

Agriculture is a critical sector where modern ways of farming are needed to accelerate the climate change goals. Over 7 lakh hectares of farmland are now covered under micro-irrigation, made possible by targeted execution of the Central schemes and greater awareness among the farmers to adopt the best practices. The Indian farmers have set examples for the world by taking measures which are in sync with the global demand to cut down carbon emissions.

The International Solar Alliance, headquartered in India, is equally playing the role of a catalyst to accelerate the efforts for energy transition. India is on course to source most of its energy needs from renewable sources. Farmers have also shown greater interest in solar pumping sets, which are also supported by the Central scheme.

India has demonstrated that behavioural changes can make substantial contributions in tackling climate change. The people have shown that they can adapt to climate-appropriate practices. India is truly living the guiding philosophy of 'Vasudhev Kutumbkam' (the world is one family).

Prime Minister Narendra Modi addressed the US Congress on 22 June 2023. This was the second occasion that PM Modi addressed the US Congress. India's G20 presidency brought global focus on the country as India has become a voice of the Global South.

The world order is in a flux. The global community is facing a host of challenges and they require urgent attention. Disruptive technologies, financial inequity, healthcare access, climate change, pandemic response, global response, energy transition, etc., are some of the issues currently at the top of the global agenda. India has shown leadership in all the global issues including advocating peace efforts in the ongoing Russia–Ukraine conflict.

India, in the last financial year, registered 7.2 per cent GDP growth. The first quarter GDP growth was 7.8 per cent in 2023–24.[4] India has once more come out as the fastest growing economy in the world. By becoming the fifth largest economy in the world, India is being sought after by the developed world. India has regularly been taking part in the G7 meetings. Indian economy in fact is bigger than four of the G7 countries. Thus, India is being accorded a pivotal position in global economic affairs.

It must also be mentioned that Indian voice on issues such as climate change is heard with all seriousness. By forming International Solar Alliance, India has shown the roadmap for clean energy transition to achieve the goal of net zero emissions. At the same time, India raised the voice of the Global South and the poor countries strongly at the Hiroshima summit of the G7 meeting.

At such a juncture, it's important to keep tabs on the Indian political leaders and their responses to prepare a collective response for the country on such global challenges. In the matters of international affairs, India for decades has had a consensus among political leaders to speak in one voice. This unity served the national interests of the country well in times when India faced challenges.

Late Atal Bihari Vajpayee spoke for India when he was abroad as an Opposition leader. Former Congress president Rahul Gandhi needs to know that when he attempts to belittle PM Modi during his foreign visits, he actually ends up harming Indian interests.

Today, the Opposition needs to introspect if it has been able to play a constructive role in responding to issues which are of grave importance. By falling for the greed to spread disinformation, the Opposition does more harm to Indian interests and even harms credibility in people's eyes.

India came out with two vaccines when the world was battling the COVID-19 pandemic. PM Modi made it clear that the Indian vaccines are for the people of the world. When the developed world was stocking the vaccines, India was sending them to the poor countries who could not have bought costly doses of the multinational companies. India not only vaccinated her own population but also provided the protective shield to millions of people the world over. Even during the pandemic outbreak, the Opposition could not play a constructive role. The Opposition had run a campaign against India's vaccine diplomacy. But India won the hearts of the people all over the world, and the goodwill gained now serves the national interests of the country.

Opposition for the sake of opposition makes for bad politics. Parliamentary committees provide platforms for the members of the Opposition parties to become equal stakeholders in formulating the country's response to key challenges.

Artificial intelligence (AI) is one such disruptive technology. AI is being widely debated in parliaments of developed countries. The Opposition in our country should also come forward and share their views on the issue which can be considered by the government.

On global issues, it is desirable that India should speak in one voice. When PM Modi would address the US Congress for the second time in his tenure as the prime minister of the country, the world will be looking at him with hope that India will be able to provide solutions to several challenges faced by global humanity. The global hope from India is also because the country rushed food grains to other countries which faced acute hunger crisis after the outbreak of the Russia–Ukraine conflict. PM Modi, in equal measures, told both Russian president Vladimir Putin and his Ukrainian counterpart Volodymyr Zelenskyy that only diplomacy is the way out of war.

The record FDI flow in the country shows that the world truly believes in the Indian economy. Trained Indian manpower is being sought after in the Middle East,

Europe, Taiwan, the US and Australia. The emergence of India as a global power is also being welcomed by people across the world as they know that India has always positively contributed to global humanity. This calls for the Opposition parties to sit back and reflect as well as introspect.

7

Farmers First for Modi

Prime Minister Narendra Modi during a visit to Deoghar, Jharkhand

With Prime Minister Narendra Modi at the helm of the government, price rise ceased to be an election issue. Price rise issue used to be a mainstay in most of the elections. From the first election to 2014 Lok Sabha polls, price rise invariably gained limelight. Slogans around price rise would be mostly heard in the election rallies.

But the Modi government gained firm control over the price rise issue. Policies were put in place to encourage higher production of essential commodities which occasionally faced shortages. Policies were also adjusted to ensure that people felt no need to hoard essential goods. The marketplace eco-system became dynamic to allow faster transport of goods.

The efforts to create an agricultural marketplace through e-NAM and by nudging the state governments to undertake the Agricultural Produce Marketing Cooperatives (APMC) Act for the larger benefits of farmers and consumers proved instrumental in locking the issue of price rise in the political history books.

An example to show the manner in which the Modi government gained control over the issue of price rise is tur dal (pulses). It was often seen that the prices of pulses would soar some months before the Modi government took the office. India was a net importer of pulses until then, with the country sourcing pulses from places such as African countries and Myanmar. While the domestic demand for pulses was to the extent of 23 million tonne, India was producing about 16–17 million tonnes, and thus creating a shortfall.

The Modi government decided to close the chapter on the issue of price rise of pulses once for all. In place of letting the prevailing system of allowing foreign countries to gain from the national resources, the Modi government decided that the Indian farmers should benefit. The minimum support prices (MSPs) for pulses were given historical rise in 2015 and thereafter.

The MSP for tur dal, for instance, in 2014 agricultural marketing season was ₹4,350 per tonne. The MSP for tur dal for 2023 was ₹7,000. This translates into over 60 per cent increase in the MSPs for the main staple in Indian food. The Modi government in a similar way effected historic increase in the MSPs for wheat, paddy, oilseeds, besides supporting prices for sugarcane.

The farmers got the message that the Modi government is most sensitive to them. The Modi government has schemes such as Pradhan Mantri Kisan Nidhi, whereby each farmer gets ₹2,000 every four months in the bank account directly cared for by the agrarian community with message that the national resources are dedicated for their well-being. The farmers responded by working hard on the field, and India continues to produce record food grains.

Even while the world faced food shortage in the wake of the Russia–Ukraine conflict, India was resilient with record food grain production. India sent wheat consignments to countries battling hunger during the peak of the food shortage in 2021 and 2022, while continuing with the humanitarian assistance even now.

Within one year of becoming prime minister for the second term, Narendra Modi faced crises of extraordinary magnitude that the world had not faced for over 100 years. The COVID-19 pandemic had spread all over the world after breaking out from Wuhan province in China. Within months, the pandemic spread across India.

PM Modi acted with speed to save the lives of the people. The world was yet to discover a vaccine for the coronavirus. The only option before the country was to cut down the transmission of the virus. This was possible only by enforcing national lockdown.

Over a billion people in the country went under national lockdown. PM Modi took measures to protect the people against food crisis and price rise. The government led by him at the Centre ensured that 80 crore people in the country received free food grains. This ensured that there was no price rise for food grains, and all scope for hoarders to benefit from the crisis was closed.

The free food grains ensured that the poor people, who may have lost their livelihoods because of the lockdown and the subsequent staggered opening of the economy, had not to worry about food. The government took care of the food needs of the people.

Even the middle class found that there was no food price rise in the country. The Modi government paid utmost importance to agriculture, and the farmers in the country worked hard to ensure that agricultural output remained robust even during the peak of the pandemic.

The Modi government stood out with its economic intervention to deal with the pandemic. Unlike the western countries where governments printed cash to give dole outs to the people in the name of dealing with the economic disruptions, PM Modi acted with speed to insulate the poor from the crisis and targeted the vulnerable sections of society with steps to ensure that they don't face hardships.

This resulted in contrasting cases of the West still battling high inflation, making their Central banks raise interest rates. Europe is now battling recession-like situations. The US too is facing a major economic slowdown because of high inflation and high interest rates.

The Russia–Ukraine conflict brought supply-side constraints, and India also imported inflation for no fault of its own. Yet, the Modi government ensured that inflation remained only a number and did not touch the lives of the poor. The efforts of the Modi government quickly brought inflation under control, which has now gone below 5 per cent. At the same time, there is a consumption boom in the country, which can be seen in record sales of housing and cars and two-wheelers. This was made possible by the Modi government curbing price rise to allow people to gain from disposable incomes.

An honest government with zero tolerance for hoarders and black marketeers along with pro-farmer policy ecosystem freed India from the usual affairs of the prices of essential commodities climbing sharply.

The Union budget 2023–24 set the template for the economy to take firm ground in the country, empowering all sections of society including the farmers. The budget paved the way for the progress of every sector and every class. It focused on being all-inclusive and aiming to elevate the strong foundation of self-reliant India. Under the able leadership of Prime Minister Narendra Modi and Finance Minister Nirmala Sitharaman, the budget stuck to the mantra of *sabka saath, sabka vikas, sabka vishwas* and *sabka prayas*. In this Union budget, while on the one hand attention has been paid to the integrated welfare of all at the micro-economic level, on the other hand arrangements have been made to emphasize the growth of the macro-economic level.

Entering India's Amrit Kaal for the next twenty-five years, the four priorities on which development has been emphasized in the budget will lead to a self-reliant India as well as a strong and prosperous India. This budget will benefit every section of society. The biggest grain storage has been planned. This is the centre of rural development and digital payments will be seen in the agriculture sector as well. Apart from providing employment to a large population, this budget will boost the ease of living. This first budget of Amrit Kaal is going to provide the basis for fulfilling the resolution of a self-reliant and developed India. The budget will fulfil the dreams of society's aspirations as it brings revolutionary proposals for farmers and the middle class. The deprived sections have been given priority in the budget. The budget's driving force reflects the efficient and visionary leadership of Prime Minister Narendra Modi.

This budget reflects our stable economy, the power of young India and our multicultural work ethic. This budget has brought rays of development to the last man, reflecting the vision of our government. This budget is going to emphasize education, earning and well-being. The new income tax exemption limit will benefit the middle class. Pensioners, family pensioners and people getting fixed salaries will get relief from the standard deduction in the new system. In 2002, the limit of income tax exemption for non-government salaried employees in leave encashment on retirement was fixed at 3 lakh rupees. At that time, the highest basic pay in the government was ₹30,000. This limit is being increased to ₹25 lakh. That is, there will be no tax on leave encashment up to ₹25 lakh.[1]

Start-ups in the agriculture sector will increase. The agricultural loan target is being increased to ₹20 lakh crore. Agritech start-ups will grow with the Agriculture Accelerator Fund. This will help the farmers and they will be able to face challenges easily. This will increase productivity. It will be between farmers, state and industry partner. Agriculture credit target has been increased to ₹20 lakh crore with focus on animal husbandry, dairy and fisheries. In the next three years, 1 crore farmers will be encouraged to practice natural farming. Ten thousand bio-input research centres will be established. For this, emphasis will be given on micro fertilizer. A total of ₹1,564 crore has been allocated in the Union budget 2023–24 for census 2021 and its related exercise. Census activities have been stalled for more than three years due to the coronavirus epidemic.

The allocation for the census exercise is less than half the new amount compared to ₹3,676 crore in last year's budget estimates. Thus, every penny is being taken care of and the budget will usher in a new era of development, India a self-reliant nation. The government has provided a capital outlay of ₹2.40 lakh crore for the railway sector. This is nine times more than the budget of 2013-14. Capital business has increased with special emphasis on roads and highways, railways, housing and urban works. This will directly affect the economic development of the country. In the budget, the budget of the Central government's biggest housing scheme for the poor has been increased by 66 per cent.[2] The budget will create a strong foundation to fulfil the grand vision of a developed India. This budget gives priority to the underprivileged. This budget will fulfil the dreams of everyone in the village, from poor section to farmers and middle class.

PM's Vishwakarma Kaushal Samman will bring a big change in the lives of crores of *vishwakarmas* (workers). Traditionally in our country, one must create something by working hard with their own hands, tools and equipment. An ambitious scheme to form new primary co-operatives has also been announced in the budget. After this budget, digital payments will be made available to agriculture sector. Therefore, in this budget, we have come up with a very big plan for digital agriculture infrastructure. The drive for credit support and reforms for our industries has been taken forward. The middle class is a huge force to fulfil the dreams of a prosperous and developed India.

The agrarian reforms tried by the government through three farm laws sought to empower the farmers to help them realize the remunerative prices for their produces. It was unfortunate that the three agriculture reform bills brought by the Centre were not taken in the right spirit and proper perspective by a section of farmers, particularly in Punjab and Haryana, and an undue protest was staged without understanding the reformist spirit and importance of the bills.

Punjab is known for being the sword arm as well as food grain granary of India. After Independence, the country started facing a shortage of food grains, so much so that we had to beg for food grains on the international stage to meet our requirements. Then a slew of massive yet revolutionary measures were taken in the agrarian sector aimed at increasing the production of food grains, and in due course, it took the shape of a green revolution. The results of these steps were very positive and progressive, and in a span of ten years, India became a self-reliant food economy. It not only became self-sufficient but also a surplus food economy. The staple of the green revolution includes the use of the high yielding variety (HYV) of seeds, irrigation, chemical fertilizers and pesticides, etc. When the steps for the green revolution were being implemented, many people and scholars raised their concerns regarding these drastic steps and its impact on the ecology and cropping patterns of the state.

The green revolution is claimed as a great success. There is no doubt that it has some loopholes. It led to interpersonal, urban, rural and interregional inequality in food grain production and farmers into repetitive cropping patterns that led to degradation of soil and excessive exploitation of the land, increasing desertification of soil in Punjab. The overuse of water led to fall in the water table since HYV required a comparatively very high amount of water for irrigation. Excessive and uncontrolled use of chemical fertilizers, pesticides and herbicides degraded the environment by increasing pollution levels in land, water and air. Overuse of chemical pesticides and weedicides has resulted in toxicity of oil and food. It has also led to a problem of abundance and lack of quality of the crops.

India became self-sufficient since we saw 250 per cent growth in food production after the green revolution. These steps were like input costs or output linkages. Farmers' boosters for recovering the ailing agrarian sector were given a minimum guaranteed price (MSP) at which their produce would be procured by the government through Agricultural Produce and Livestock Market Committee (APMC). Also, the farmers were given input subsidies like fertilizer subsidy, free power and other facilities. By 1970, Punjab was producing 70 per cent of the country's total food.[3]

But the growth of agriculture reached stagnation and hit a plateau in the mid-1970s. As per a study by the leading university of the state, this agrarian crisis worsened in the 1990s. It started worsening so much so that in FY 2018–19, the percentage of GDP produced by the agricultural sector in Punjab's economy was just 25 per cent in FY 2018–19[4] with a meagre growth rate of the agricultural sector at 2.3 per cent. Punjab ranked first in GDP per capita amongst Indian states in 1981, which declined to fourth in 2001 but has experienced slower growth than the rest of India, having the second-lowest GDP per capita growth rate of all Indian states and UTs between 2000 and 2010, behind only Manipur. In 2019–20, Punjab drifted down from rank 17 to rank 19 in terms of per capita GDP.[5] As per a study conducted by the leading universities of the state, a total of 16,606 farmers and farm labourers committed suicide between 2000 and 2015, which equals to 3 suicides per day! From 2015–20, there were no farm laws, still the farmers were committing suicide and 95 per cent of them were debt-ridden.[6]

Thus, the farm laws were for restoring the health and wealth of farming in Punjab as well as across the country. But the vested interests sabotaged the well-meaning farm laws to push back the farmers on their stressed conditions where they keep on adding debts, while not benefiting from the integration with the markets fully.

8

Freeing Politics from Dynasts

Prime Minister Narendra Modi greets a delegation of Punjab leaders at his residence in New Delhi

Prime Minister Narendra Modi has shown a special bond with the people of Jammu and Kashmir. Under the leadership of PM Modi, the people of Jammu and Kashmir have felt and experienced the healing touch of the Central government, as well as a vision taking visible wings of economic prosperity. This is indeed a major relief for the people who suffered at the hands of the political dynasts. In fact, the Opposition space is full of dynasts who exhibit a sense of entitlement by ruling over several political parties as their personal fiefdom.

This is also reflected in Baramulla deputy commissioner Syed Sehrish Asgar bagging the top award for civil services, as she executed the vision of the aspirational district of PM Modi on the ground by bringing the gains of the Central schemes to the people in proactive manner. No wonder that the people in Jammu and Kashmir have begun believing in PM Modi's mantra of *sabka saath, sabka vikas*.

A close examination of the ninety-nine episodes of PM Modi's monthly radio broadcast Mann Ki Baat reveals that Jammu and Kashmir has always been at the core of his conversations with the people. There have been numerous accounts of the people which found mention from PM Modi.

It has been an earnest resolve of the Central government that democracy at the grassroots take strong roots in Jammu and Kashmir. This alone can ensure sustainable development and the participation of the people in the journey of progress of the Union territory, as well as India. The overwhelming participation of hundreds of people in the panchayat elections in Jammu and Kashmir firmly endorses PM Modi's vision for the UT.

People across the world, including India, have curiosity about Jammu and Kashmir. PM Modi by sharing the stories of the people of the UT in his radio broadcast regularly has kept the world updated about the marching progress of the UT and the deepening participation of democracy and partaking by the people in the gains of development.

The entrepreneurial journey of Abdul Majeed Wani, who took to e-commerce to sell GI-tagged saffron at a Pampore trading centre, found mention in Mann Ki Baat. The historical significance of Kashmiri saffron was brought before the global audience. Saffron indeed is the identity of Jammu and Kashmir. The most sought-after commodity is also the source of livelihood of the local people, and PM Modi gave it global scale by making a special mention in Mann ki Baat.

Javed Ahmed had survived a terrorist attack in the Kashmir Valley in 1996. He now has dedicated his life to improving infrastructure for the specially challenged people in the Valley. His life is for humanity and an example of selfless service to society. PM Modi showered praise on him as he is an example for everyone. Besides, he proved to be a reason for an elaborate thoughtful reflection by the top leadership of the country on the issue of ease of access of public places for the specially challenged people.

Balbir Kaur, the sarpanch of Gram Treva in Jammu, who constructed a thirty-bed quarantine centre and made arrangements for water on roads leading to the panchayat, also found mention in Mann ki Baat. This again was an acknowledgement of efforts at the local body level for the well-being of the people.

Zaitoona Begum, a sarpanch, decided that her panchayat would fight against the coronavirus pandemic while also creating income opportunities for the local people. She distributed free masks and free rations as well as crop seeds and apple saplings so that people could be effectively empowered. The world got to know her after she found mention in Mann ki Baat.

Mohd Iqbal, municipal president of Anantnag, too found mention in the radio programme for his feat of designing a sprayer machine at a cost of ₹50,000, while the machine if brought from another town would have cost ₹6 lakh. By mentioning him in Mann ki Baat, PM Modi lauded individual efforts of finding local solutions with innovations.

In fact, Jammu and Kashmir has regularly been featuring in the radio broadcasts to show that PM Modi is closely following the developments in the UT. In one such mention, PM Modi stated that the people of Pulwama, including Manzoor Ahmad Alai, have shown entrepreneurship skills. Alai sold his ancestral land to establish a unit for manufacturing wooden boxes and later expanded his business to include supplying pencil slats to big companies. His business is now worth crores and provides livelihood to around 200 people.

Srinagar Municipal Corporation, which appointed Bilal Dar, an eighteen-year-old from Srinagar, as the brand ambassador for the *swachhata abhiyan*, too was lauded. Also, Manzoor Ahmed Larhwal from Srinagar, who installed a solar rooftop plant to cut down electricity bills, was lauded by PM Modi.

Similarly, Vinod Kumar from Palli village of Jammu, who has been beekeeping in more than 15,000 colonies, also featured along with cyclist Adil Altaf from Srinagar, who bagged laurels. Muhammad Aslam from Shopian, Jammu and Kashmir, who played a role in organizing the community mobilization programme 'Back to Village' too was appreciated by PM Modi.

Abrogation of Article 370 paved way for a new era of peace and prosperity in Jammu and Kashmir. In the past, Jammu and Kashmir was known as the epicentre of terrorism in the country. But it has now become a tourism capital, where people from all parts of the country come and boost the economy of the region. In 2022, maximum number of tourists came to Jammu and Kashmir, surpassing the past record arrivals in the last seventy years. International-level successful events were held in Jammu and Kashmir, showing the peace and development of Jammu and Kashmir to the world community.

Since the abrogation of Article 370, incidents of cross-border firing have become negligible, while the ISI game plan has been defeated. Children are no longer talking about bricks and stones but are looking for computers and books. A positive environment of education has been created for students in schools and colleges.

A new era of development has come to Jammu and Kashmir under the guidance of Prime Minister Narendra Modi, where all sections of society are progressing. There is no discrimination against any section of society, whether it is Gujjar or Bakarwal. The economy of Jammu and Kashmir has reached a new height and people have started looking for a better life beyond the Abdullahs and Muftis who exploited Jammu and Kashmir for decades to promote family interests. The weaker sections of society, who were deprived of their rights before the abrogation of Article 370, are now gaining the benefits of all the schemes of the Central government. For the past many decades, the Abdullahs and Muftis were engaged in politics of self-interests. On their watch, women of Jammu and Kashmir suffered, while tribal population, including Paharis, Valmakis, SCs, STs and West Pakistan refugees, was deprived of their rights. They have been misleading the people of Jammu and Kashmir with their slogan of justice. Article 370 has been the biggest hindrance to the development of Jammu and Kashmir, especially the weaker sections.

Many public welfare steps have been taken up for the people of Jammu and Kashmir ever since Article 370 was done away with, and a new era has dawned upon the union territory. Jammu and Kashmir has moved away from terrorism to tourism, from bullets and stones to new education and development. People have realized how the Abdullahs and Muftis kept them in the dark all these years and played to the tunes of Pakistan's ISI to deprive people of development and progress.

By abstaining from the programme of PM Modi, KCR shows arrogance, besides becoming a barrier for PM Modi meeting the people of Telangana. The discomfort of KCR is because of his family-oriented politics, which is deeply involved in corruption.

KCR cannot see PM Modi in his eyes. It's a serious lapse on the part of KCR that he slips away whenever PM Modi visits Telangana. His utter disrespect to protocol as laid out by the Constitution is a sign of deep nervousness. PM Modi is welcomed by the people across the country with open hearts. The joy among the people of Telangana whenever PM Modi visits the state can be seen on the street.

KCR has overseen one of the most corrupt regimes in any of the states in the country. The paper leaks of examinations in Telangana are a new normal. The papers of the public service commission also get leaked. Such leaked papers make rounds on WhatsApp of the people summarily.

BJP's former state chief Bandi Sanjay had also received one such leaked paper on his WhatsApp, as had been the case with several other politicians. The people in the state have legitimate concerns that mafias run Telangana, where corruption is the only means to move forward in all walks of life. Bandi Sanjay being a committed soldier of the BJP, who is devoted to the well-being of the people, has been agitating in Telangana against the rampant corruption by KCR and his government.

Liquor mafia runs the show in Telangana. The state government has been found wanting to act against the liquor mafia. This is now unravelling, as the Enforcement Directorate (ED) is going to the depths of the nexus of the politicians with the liquor mafia.

9

Pain of Punjab

Prime Minister Narendra Modi chairing the 7th Governing Council meeting of the Niti Aayog in New Delhi

The crisis in Punjab has been likened to the concept of a state of nature described by Thomas Hobbes – a society without a functioning government, where life is 'nasty, brutish and short'. This comparison paints a grim picture of Punjab's current predicament, where various issues have converged to create a pervasive crisis affecting different aspects of the state's well-being.

Punjab, often referred to as the 'food bowl of India', finds itself in the midst of a multifaceted crisis. Law and order have deteriorated to alarming levels with rising crime rates, daily murders, looting and ransom calls. The situation has become so dire that even the headquarters of Punjab's intelligence agency was targeted, illustrating the lack of safety and control. This deterioration can be attributed to a lack of clear direction, vision and effective policy goals from the current government.

Furthermore, the economic landscape of Punjab is bleak. Once considered one of India's richest states in terms of per capita income, Punjab now grapples with a sinking economy. Ill-advised economic decisions and populist measures have worsened the financial situation, leading to a mounting debt burden. The state's outstanding debt is projected to increase substantially, and the government is resorting to borrowing money just to pay off interest on existing loans. These economic challenges have been compounded by unrealistic promises made by the political administration, adding to the disillusionment among the people.

The economy of Punjab is painting a state of classical debt trap where the state's outstanding debt is projected to increase from ₹2.83 to ₹3.05 lakh crore in FY 2022–23.[1] Each Punjabi has a per capita debt of 1 lakh rupees which makes it one of the worst managed economies among the Indian states. Agriculture sector has reached its saturation, and now there is hardly any scope for expansion in this sector. Poor farmers and peasants are under debt and the instances of their committing suicide are rising. The current political class blames everything on either the earlier regime or the Centre instead of coming up with a viable alternative.

Amidst this crisis, there are disturbing trends emerging. Extremist forces are gaining traction, exploiting unmet expectations among the youth. The rise of such elements poses a threat to national unity, utilizing religious platforms to further their secessionist agenda. Additionally, Punjab is grappling with narco-terrorism, with the proliferation of drug-related issues exacerbated by lacklustre efforts to combat the problem at an institutional level.

The political landscape is marked by confusion and lack of leadership. The chief minister's perceived detachment from the state's issues, including instances of remote control from Delhi, has raised concerns about effective governance. The government's actions and policies have fallen short, leaving Punjab in a state of turmoil.

The current regime is just for projection instead of working for action. There is no direction, vision or goal. The state political regime is on a compulsive, conflicting path with the Centre. Instead of protecting the interests of Punjabis, it is being dictated, remote controlled and managed by the party from Delhi. This is leading to sacrificing the interests of Punjab for the sake of Delhi.

Every now and then, Punjab is gripped by a payment crisis. Drug abuse is the highest in the region. There is no industrial policy. Industry is shifting to other states because of lack of infrastructure and a clear vision. The cost of freebies is being shifted, burdening the industry. How can any industry survive in this situation?

The bureaucracy is indecisive since the political dispensation lacks direction and vision. Most senior bureaucrats are seeking Central deputation. The policies and their execution are tardy and lack implementation.

Punjab's crisis spans various domains – from law and order to the economy, extremism and political leadership. It is imperative for comprehensive and effective measures to be taken to address these challenges and lead the state towards stability and progress.

Law and order situation in Punjab has completely collapsed. There is a serious sense of fear and panic among the people in the state. The Aam Aadmi Party-led Punjab government is giving out fake figures of police actions against criminals amid rising hopelessness among the people. Punjab has seen three serious incidents of looting in quick succession.

In one incident, ₹8.5 crore were looted by criminals in Ludhiana on 10 June[2] and ₹10.5 lakh was looted in Amritsar a day after. This was followed by yet another killing and looting at the shop of a jeweller in Moga. The prevailing situation in the state reflects poorly on the Punjab Police, which had played a commendable role in fighting militancy but is now being used by the AAP government to cover up its failures on all fronts.

Prisons in Punjab have become the playground of criminals and sharpshooters. The writ of the law is hardly seen running in Punjab. This calls for an urgent intervention from the stakeholders. There are signs in Punjab showing that the AAP government has converted prisons into channel studios for hardened criminals. Gangster Lawrence Bishnoi has managed to give interviews to the media from the high-security cells of a jail. The manner in which Lawrence Bishnoi has been able to give interviews from prison reveals that law and order is gasping for breath in Punjab. There is no denying that law and order situation in Punjab has completely collapsed in the past few months.

One can easily make out that the prisoners have all the means of communication within their prison cells to run their cartels across the state. The business of extortion is flourishing in Punjab. Gangsters' access to all facilities in prison cells to carry out criminal activities reveals that Bhagwant Mann, who as chief minister of Punjab has completed more than one year in the office, has not only failed, but he's seen with bloodied nose as an administrator.

It needs no reiteration that Punjab is a state with an international border. Memories are still fresh that Pakistan waged a failed proxy war with India in Punjab by sponsoring terrorism in the 1980s. It is also well documented by researchers and even investigative agencies that Pakistan continues to wage proxy war against India in Punjab by exporting arms and drugs through drones and other means. At the same time, it needs no explanation that Pakistan is orchestrating an international conspiracy to radicalize the Punjabi diaspora with the Khalistani agenda with an aim to seek revenge from India for the liberation of Bangladesh.

The background and perspective of Punjab must have been known to the AAP. Arvind Kejriwal, the national co-convenor of the AAP, has been a chief minister for quite a long time and is familiar with the challenges of Punjab. Yet, Kejriwal allowed Mann to remain aloof from the day-to-day functioning of the state administration.

This is worrisome. Even after the sharp observations of the Supreme Court against officials who have been specifically named for the lapses in the security of Prime

Minister Narendra Modi during his visit to Punjab when Charanjeet Singh Channi was the chief minister, the Mann government sat over the recommendations for tough actions against the top officials. This was demoralizing for the police, which is incumbent on strict compliance with the laid-down standard operating procedures (SOP). The sense that the security of the prime minister could be compromised and none would be held accountable emboldened the armed gangsters and the hardened criminals.

Industrialists and businessmen dread phone calls. The business of extortion is gaining ground with each passing day. This can also be seen from the fact that the Punjab-based industrialists are visiting states such as Uttar Pradesh in search of investment opportunities. The revenue collections in Punjab have also gone down. This suggests that the poor law and order situation in Punjab is also pushing the state economy down. This is the reason why Punjab has one of the highest unemployment rates in the country among the youth.

Punjab's own tax revenue has decreased from 71.82 per cent from 2011–12 to 47.79 per cent in 2021–22.[3] This shows a clear decline in the state's ability to raise resources internally, while Punjab is now banking on transfers and debts from the Union government. The declining mobilization of resources from within Punjab also reveals that the poor law and order situation now has a telling effect on the state of affairs of the economy.

Also, the Punjab economy is lagging behind states with better administrative records. While the state GDP growth in the current fiscal year is pegged to grow at 9.5 per cent at a nominal rate, the same for Uttar Pradesh is projected at 19 per cent, while being 15 per cent for Assam. The declining revenue of the state government is also pushing Punjab further into debt trap.

Effective outstanding debt to gross state domestic product (GSDP) of Punjab has been estimated to be 46.81 per cent for FY 2023–24, while effective outstanding debt to GSDP of Punjab was estimated to be 45.23 per cent for FY 2022–23. Outstanding debt of Punjab as per the budget estimates for FY 2023–24 is ₹3,47,542.39 crore. The debt paid in 2022–23 was ₹30,046 crore, while the borrowing for 2022–23 (as per the budget) was ₹55,051 crore. Debt to be paid in 2023–24 is ₹38,626 crore, while the borrowing for 2023–24 (budgeted) is ₹94,410 crore.

Thus, it is evident that Punjab is borrowing more to pay the heavy price for the collapse of the law-and-order situation in the state.

10

Rahul and Mamata with Divisive Elements

Prime Minister Narendra Modi at the Red Fort on the occasion of India's 76th Independence Day

Ideology is the basis on which any political party works. This gives a purpose for which a party is to function and aim for power. The grand old party of India led the multi-regional, multi-people and multi-community freedom struggle. To quote Bipan Chandra, the famous leftist historian, Congress during freedom struggle was not a political party but an umbrella movement in which different ideologies merged to fight for nationalism.

Over the last two decades, the nation has witnessed a slow and incremental collapse of the ideological roots of the Congress party. The ideology of the Congress which should be the basis of any political outfit has been replaced with an ideology which is diametrically opposite of the very philosophy for which it was formed. Congress since Independence has claimed to believe in the philosophy of secularism, Fabian-socialism and national integration.

Congress has claimed to be championing the cause of national integration and sovereignty and unity in India as its core ideological ethos. For Congress, secularism means 'Sarva Dharma Sama Bhava', collectively termed by its party members as secularism. The slogan '*Bharat tere tukde honge*; Insha Allah, Insha Allah' grabbed the attention of the nation during the 2016 JNU sedition row. It got hyped and earned notoriety as a war cry against the very national integration of the Indian nation by the left-leaning anarchist group of so-called students. The meaning of this slogan is – India, you will be divided into pieces as per the will of Allah.

This provocative and highly anti-national slogan was raised at JNU to protest against the hanging of Afzal Guru, who was convicted by the Hon'ble Supreme Court for abetting and aiding terrorists in India and waging war against the Indian nation. This slogan was also ideologically supported by many a 'left-liberal-intellectuals' as well as the main Centrist ideologically political outfit, Congress. There were a few leaders of political outfits who had visited the JNU campus in February 2016 to express solidarity with the students. This protest was led by Kanhaiya Kumar, the president of the JNU Students' Union and national leader of the All India Students Federation (AISF).

After that, he joined the Communist Party of India (CPI) and served as a National Executive Council member of CPI. This former CPI leader was welcomed into the fold of Indian National Congress on 28 September 2021. In politics, persons do not matter, 'ideas' matter. Kanhaiya Kumar may have joined as an individual and he has all the right to join any political outfit. But the ideology he represents is communist, leftist and negative. It is dangerous, poisonous and toxic for the health and well-being of India.

He ideologically supported Afzal Guru who was a threat to our nation and was convicted by the very guardian of the Constitution, the Hon'ble Supreme Court of India. These anti-India slogans were justified even on the grounds of freedom of speech and freedom of expression. What can be more than the nadir of ideology than using one's ideology to subvert the very nation for which it was idealized? Is it thinkable that you can support 'Laden' in the USA?

If you look at the slogan '*Bharat tere tukde honge*', on the face of it, it seems that this slogan is just a provocative, anti-India slogan, but that is just a superfluous understanding. This is not merely a slogan but an ideology that is giving birth to these kinds of slogans. This slogan is just a superstructure which is standing on a substructure of an ideology, which is detrimental to the very existence of this nation. At the outset, we should understand what the ideological roots of this underlying ideology are?

This slogan was chanted by the ideologues of the 'leftist-Marxists-liberals' whose citadel is JNU. The communist ideology is a hypothesis which was propagated by its proponent, Karl Marx. Their basic assumption is that the moving force of human progress is 'matter' and not 'idea'. It assumes material or economic factors as the basis of change and development and other factors like religion, nationalism and ideology are just the shadow of the prevailing economic relationships, which they purportedly divide between the rich and the poor, the haves and the have-nots, the capitalist bourgeoisie and the labour proletariats. Nationalism and nation-state are 'false consciousness' among the masses projected by the rich to control the 'minds' of the poor and perpetuate the former's control!

Only by throwing away the yoke of religion and nationalism, the so-called state of classless and stateless society would emerge through violence and revolution. Of late, the neo-left liberals of India have also started believing in libertarianism, individualism and constitutionalism and claim to believe in equality, human rights, rule of law, women emancipation, etc. So this ideology of the Indian leftists in which Kanhaiya Kumar has been groomed is an extreme anti-nation ideology. He represents that ideology and ironically has surfaced as a symbol of that ideology.

The ultimate aim of communism is ending the nation-state through wresting the power of government and creating a utopian state of 'classless, stateless society'. Imagine, the philosophy whose very basic is to overthrow the nation-state through violent means how dangerous it will prove for our nation. People like Kanhaiya claim to oppose the government in power, but in the garb of opposing the government, they oppose the very country and nation. They do not desist from spreading and promoting the ideas of secession, anti-nationalism and anarchy. They will find fault in anything and everything which is the idea of 'India'. They disrespect the sovereignty of India and its national symbols, be it the very unity of India, its national flag, its armed-forces or any other. Since their prime aim is to destroy the very nation-state itself, they build up their 'narratives' of anti-India, be it its historical past or the present or the progress of the nation in future.

Even the history of India is interpreted from this so-called perspective where the glorious and historical achievements are ridiculed and distorted. They hail secession, separatism and anti-nationalism in India. Chants like '*Bharat tere tukde tukde honge*' and '*Bharat teri barbadi*' are just a reflection of their ideological grooming of anti-nationalism. The ageing Congress, in its quest to regain its lost base, has compromised its ideological stands. It has included in its lap people from ideological extremes like these who are against the very ideological ethos of the grand but dying old party of India. Either the 'revolution' of Kanhaiya has been compromised or the 'ideology' of the Congress. It is not a lone incident.

The musings by the political advisors of the former Punjab Congress chief Navjot Singh Sidhu on Kashmir and Pakistan clearly say that Congress, in its desperation, has forgotten the ideals of its founders.

The general election to the legislative assembly of the eastern state of West Bengal for 292 constituencies of the 294 constituencies concluded on 29 April 2021. The much-awaited and hyped result of these polls was out on 2 May. In this biggest show of democracy in recent years, close to 6 crore people voted with an average voting percentage of 81.87 per cent.

There were many issues on which elections were fought. The mismanagement and lack of development under the aegis of the Trinamool Congress, issues of refugees, appeasement of certain sections of society on religious lines and politically motivated violence against opponents with the support of state apparatus were a few of them. The notable patterns which emerged out of these elections have a bearing on the future political spectrum of India. Out of 292 seats, Congress did not win even a single seat. It is worth reminding that the Trinamool Congress has its origins in the Congress when Mamta Banerjee split from the Congress and formed her own regional party. From 2 Lok Sabha seats and 5.5 per cent votes in Lok Sabha elections in 2019, and 44 MLA seats in previous assembly elections, the Congress is reduced to zero by just getting 2.94 per cent votes! So much so, its family chieftain, Rahul Gandhi, could not muster the courage to do even a single rally in the first four phases of the election in West Bengal.

It was also a blow to the last dying citadel of the left where CPI and CPM both fought together along with the Congress. Both CPI and CPM are reduced to zero seats with CPM getting only 4.73 per cent votes. Imagine a party that held the communist bastion for five decades when in the whole world communism is reduced to a non-entity. BJP has many gains to its credit.

Firstly, it is the BJP which has dislodged the left and the Congress, replacing them and taking their place as the main and the only Opposition party. In the 2011 assembly election, BJP had failed to open its account and got just 4 per cent vote share. In the 2016 assembly election, BJP bagged three seats and got 10 per cent vote share. In the current election, it has won seventy-seven seats – a massive and gigantic increase of seventy-four seats. It has polled 38.13 per cent vote share – a jump of 28.13 per cent from the 2016 MLA elections. It was able to defeat the very face and façade of TMC, Mamata Banerjee, by its candidate Suvendu Adhikari from Nandigram by 1956 votes in a keenly fought contest.

It was the biggest ever blow to the TMC, which is unparallel in the electoral history of India, where the leader on the strength on which the whole election was fought got a crushing and humiliating defeat. BJP under the leadership of Modi created its own cadre, strength and leadership in the state, which can be of great help in making its presence in the coming years, more particularly in the 2024 Lok Sabha Elections. On the face of it, it seemed democracy has won. However, as the event unfolded during the polls and more specifically after the poll results, democracy was ashamed of the violence perpetrated by the ruling party to silence its political opponent.

The serious and worrisome trend is the use of violence as a political weapon by the All-India Trinamool Congress and its cadre with open, encouraging and inciting support from its leader, Mamata Banerjee.

She was clear in her approach for appeasement and pampering of minorities, which was diametrically opposite to the agenda of BJP of development and progress in Bengal and *sabka saath sabka vishwas*. Elections in any democracy are based on differences of opinion. The difference in opinion is healthy for democracy and even for democratic values. But to use state-sponsored violence to further political goals and ideology is deplorable and shameful. Never ever such a shameful and low level of politics has been witnessed in recent Indian history.

The situation is alarming where the families of Hindus who supported the BJP are fleeing the area (like in Birbhum). Torture, murder and rape of BJP supporters have become very common since the administration is assisting this genocide. It reminds us of the Direct Action Day of Jinnah's Muslim League where violence was perpetrated against the Hindus in the name of religion. This political violence by instigating communal fault lines has made everyone conclude that though AITC won the election but has failed the democracy!

Mamta Banerjee is essentially the new Jinnah in the making. Indian democracy is the largest functional and vibrant democracy in the world. The core feature of democracy is adult franchise with secret ballot so as to give a sense of security to the voters to use their voting rights in a free and fair manner. Not only a voter is free to cast his vote freely, but he also has a free atmosphere where he can decide his representative without any fear of being intimidated. Also, the major difference between a democratic and non-democratic form of government and country is the smooth transition of power from one party to another without any violence. Democracy also means non-use of violence as a means of political agenda. It is the rule of ballot over bullet. We refer to democratic means as peaceful, law-abiding means where Constitutional means are used and rule of law is supreme.

What has been happening in West Bengal post-poll is undemocratic, illegal and extra-Constitutional. It seems we have come to mediaeval, dark feudal age where those who stand against the feudal mindset are tortured, raped and brutally murdered. In her political quest to be a messiah of certain sections of population and her appeasement policy, she has stooped to a level never heard before.

Imagine a current CM appealing the minorities to vote on communal lines in elections. Mamata Banerjee in her demagogy and rhetoric against the Centre instigated the people to work against the very federal and Constitutional structure, be it her open inciting of violence against the Central Paramilitary forces who were working under the Election Commission of India (ECI), her diatribe against the ECI or her hitting and demeaning every federal institution and structure of India.

The stalling of the Durga Puja festival, especially the idol immersions, so that the Muslim community, who were incidentally having their mourning festival of Muharram at the same time, could proceed without a fuss clearly indicated her appeasement and pseudo-secular stance. This post-poll violence is not a spontaneous eruption but a well-conspired and well-crafted strategy to create an ecosystem of fear and violence, which was fuelled by Mamata Banerjee during the election campaign period.

The violence and killing of political opponents, gang-raping of women, targeting a particular community and the scene of tortured houses are forcing the people to flee and take refuge outside the state. It is nothing less than a crime against humanity. This state-sponsored violence cannot take place without the active involvement of the state administration and police, which did not act.

Even the Congress and left parties slammed the post-poll violence unleashed by TMC workers on political opponents in West Bengal and said the electorate did not vote for such lawlessness. We are reminded of Direct Action by Jinnah. Direct Action Day (16 August 1946), which is also known as the 1946 Calcutta Killings, was a day of nationwide protest by the Indian Muslim community announced by Jinnah in which communal-instigated violent attacks were made on Hindus.

Jinnah pronounced that they would either have a divided India or a destroyed India. It led to large-scale violence between Muslims and Hindus in the city of Calcutta (now known as Kolkata) in the Bengal province of British India. As Jinnah sowed the seeds of division of India on basis of communal lines, the rhetoric by Mamata is in line with the rhetoric taken up by Jinnah, which led to the unfortunate Partition of India and mayhem of division killing millions of people.

The post-poll violence led by Mamata Banerjee is nothing but a ploy to divide the secular and harmonious culture of Bengal on the basis of communal lines. It is not only dividing the country on communal lines but also 'destroying' the very idea of India of secularism, co-operative federalism and mutual coexistence. It will have large repercussions on the secular and national fabric of the idea of India in the times to come.

11

Modi: The Master Political Healer

Prime Minister Narendra Modi at a special screening of the film Swaraj

A healer is a person who ends your sufferings, turmoil and pains. There is a subtle difference between a healer and a doctor. The doctor reduces or eliminates sufferings and pains which are related to physical body. The doctor ends only physical pain; the healer heals all kinds of pains. These pains may be physical, psychological or emotional.

Sometimes, the healer-doctor has to do a surgery with the intention of curing the pain permanently so as to heal in the long run. When society develops and politics makes it move, there are bound to emerge some social, economic and political sufferings at society level.

When India started its journey post-Independence, there cropped up crises of economic development which led to sufferings of many areas, sections, regions, social groups, etc. The so-called 'Fabian-socialist' development strategy adopted by India led to intra- and inter-regional, social groups and class differences and discriminations. These cropped up in the form of many movements, upheavals and agitations. These upheavals slowly led to social unrest in the form of sociopolitical ulcers.

It is a fact that while following the path of social-economic post-Independence growth, which was not inclusive and all pervasive, we made many blunders. These emerged as political wounds, which are inflicting pains on the body politic of our nation. There were many issues, which owing to various reasons, remained unfinished and snowballed into full-fledged problems and crises. Thousands of innocent people and our brave security personnel have lost their lives protecting the 'idea of India'.

A political healer is not only who cures these political ulcers either through treatment or surgery but also by removing the alienation of the distressed sections of society who have undergone the sufferings. There were many political ulcers plaguing India since Independence. There were political diseases, infections and wounds, which remained unaddressed either deliberately or owing to the lack of political will and expertise. One of the issues in post-Independence India was the issue of Kashmir. It led to internal strife and terrorism in Kashmir Valley killing thousands of innocent people. The issue of Kashmir emerged as a big ulcer on the body politic and has led to three wars between India and Pakistan. This was mishandled in a way that it led to a political wound which slowly degenerated into a permanently bleeding political ulcer. The so-called political leaders just allowed themselves to benefit from the situation instead of addressing it.

The ulcer was perpetrated by our neighbour country to bleed India in Kashmir by sponsoring terrorism on account of incompletion of the finished agenda of India's Independence. There was a war cry by Pakistan to bleed India for 1,000 years. Thanks to the decisive, firm and out-of-the-box expertise of the master healer, Narendra Modi, the issue of Kashmir, which was draining the wealth and resources of the nation and has led to the alienation of people of Kashmir, has been solved.

Surgery of the Kashmir wound was successfully done. Further, the healing was made through massive work of development. Ask any Kashmiri Pundit who has suffered for the last thirty years and has become a refugee in their own country what healing means! So was the healing of people of Ladakh who have been ignored by the pathetic approach of the governments and were totally alienated. This healing touch worked like magic in the northeast states also.

Another issue of contention which was creating communal tension was the issue of Ram Temple. Who could have imagined that one of the most contested issues in Indian body politic would be solved without even a drop of blood? The pride of Indian culture has been restored. With the construction of Ram-Mandir, national resurrection in the form of national pride has been restored within millions of Indians, expressing satisfaction that their dream has been fulfilled and justice has been done to them.

Another area where the pride of India has been healed is in the area of reviving India's image in international affairs. With his proactive Modi doctrine, India has emerged as a key player at sub-regional, regional and global levels. The influence of India has increased in diplomatic and strategic affairs. The various evacuation operations, be it in Afghanistan or any other troubled hotspot, people of India have a hope that the government will act decisively to save them.

The worst crisis of the century for whole humanity was COVID-19. The way India addressed this virus-born calamity is exemplary. India developed its own vaccines. India has not only saved its own population with its 90 crore vaccination, which is the highest in the world. It got a distinction of conducting 2.26 crore vaccinations in a day, which in itself is a record as it tantamounts to vaccinating more than the population of Australia in a day!

This healing was not confined to India only, but the vaccination doses were given to the people of the world. India is emerging as a true global healer under the master healer.

Weber, the famous sociologist, has given a categorization of authority which he divides into three types: traditional authority, charismatic authority and legal-rational authority. A leader having traditional authority comes to power because his family or clan has always provided the group's leadership. The second type of authority is legal-rational authority which is an authority based on rational social action. The most interesting and prevalent type of authority is charismatic authority, which is the result of personal qualities of the person who exercises it. Charisma is a powerful personal quality that some people have to attract and influence other people. It corresponds to affective social action. To Weber, charisma was a revolutionary force which can bring a massive change in society through the personal attributes of the leader. The rise of a charismatic leader may well pose a threat to the existing system and lead to a dramatic change in a system.

Charisma is a certain quality of an individual personality by virtue of which he is set apart from ordinary men and treated as endowed with supernatural, superhuman or at least specifically exceptional powers or qualities, which are regarded as exemplary, and on the basis of them, the individual concerned is treated as a leader. This type of authority becomes more pronounced in times of crisis and turmoil when other types of authority seem to be failing and new forms of authority are needed.

When we say one person is a charismatic organizer, it means he works best at the things in hand in a systematic and organized way. A master organizer is a person who is a leader and who leads by example.

The other qualities of a master organizer are: they are mission-driven, creative problem solvers, invest in relationships, know how to function strategically with limited resources, demonstrate integrity and are able to communicate their vision.

They put the interests of the group first, ahead of their individual concerns. Over the last two decades, we have seen the rise of a charismatic organizer in the political arena of the nation. A new charismatic and mass-followed person emerged from a very humble background, steering the direction of the future course of the nation. Modi's charisma did not happen overnight. Neither has he enjoyed any attributes of traditional authority where you are destined to rule since you belong to the family which has been ruling. Rather, his is the reverse case.

Before embarking upon the political journey of the most followed leader of the planet, let us see what qualities he has which have made him the most charismatic organizer. One of the best attributes of an acceptable organizer is that he is always mission-driven, be it a personal life mission or a social mission. Modi has a personal mission of serving the nation and a social mission of making India the most developed country in the world. For this, he has devoted his whole life.

At the age of seventeen, he left home to travel across India. For two years he travelled across the expansive landscape of India exploring various cultures, areas and people. When he returned home, he was a changed man with a clear aim of what he wanted to achieve in life. As a pracharak of the Rashtriya Swayamsevak Sangh (RSS) and then in various capacities in RSS, he has proved his mettle of being a mission-driven, selfless and social goal-oriented organizer. Leaders have habits which make them distinct from others. He followed a very tough routine in Ahmedabad since 1972 when he became a pracharak for RSS.

His day started at 5 am and went on till late night. While continuing to shoulder different responsibilities within the sangh during the 1980s, Narendra Modi emerged as an organizer exemplar with his organizing skills. The organizer sees and finds a solution of and in every situation, be it a problem or a challenge. He has lived with bare minimum and has lived a philosophy of minimalism in his personal life. Since the master strategist locates solutions, for him working best with the existing resources which may be frugal or limited has been his core creed.

In 1987, he was destined to be the general secretary of the BJP in Gujarat. In his first task, Modi won a victory for the BJP in Ahmedabad Municipal Corporation elections for the first time ever. He also ensured that the BJP was a close second to the Congress in the 1990 Gujarat Assembly elections. In the 1995 Assembly elections, it was his organizational acumenship that ensured that BJP's vote share increased drastically, and the party won 121 seats in the Assembly.

Modi worked as the national secretary of BJP in 1995, looking after party's activities in Haryana and Himachal Pradesh. As BJP's general secretary, he worked to ensure that BJP won the 1998 Lok Sabha elections. It was in September 2001 that he moved from the all-demanding, rough and tumble of organizational services to the world of governance. This mass organizer has relationship which spreads far beyond the political spectrum in India, and he has a knack of developing personal relations with people and leaders across the globe. Integrity and honesty are fast becoming rare commodities these days particularly in social and political arenas.

Modi served almost twenty years in public life in governance, first as Chief Minister of Gujarat and then as Prime Minister of India. Credit to the personal impeccable character and sansakaras (values) imbibed by this grounded CEO of India that not even a single allegation of any wrongdoing either in personal or in public life has been levelled against him. He is the gripping orator we have seen in the recent past who can connect with the masses, knowing their pulse and pain, who captivates his audience with his simple yet effective communication skills. For the craftsman-organizer, the whole is always bigger than the part.

For him, politics is not about getting power but about serving the nation. He has sacrificed all his enjoyments of material life just with a single aim to serve the nation and party which he calls his family. 'Pracharak' is a Hindi word that literally means one who is a preacher or one who propagates. But in the RSS parlance, a pracharak is not a canvasser or a propagandist; rather, he is an individual who is inspired by the mission and objective of the sangh and dedicates his full time to this mission. RSS pracharaks are missionaries of nationalism whose sole aim is to devote their entire lives to their aim of taking India to the supreme glory and the ideals of upholding Indian culture and spreading the ideology of the Hind rastra. A pracharak is like a monk except for the orange robe.

A pracharak has a very difficult and full-time service. He lives a minimalist life where he hardly owns any material possessions. You won't find any such example in history where missionaries spread the fervour of nationalism instead of their own religion. A pracharak has to leave his home, family and job and devote his full time to spreading the ideology of RSS. So a very high level of devotion and dedication for the country is needed to become a pracharak. His day starts before the sun rises and ends late at night. For a pracharak, nation comes even before himself.

He is always ready to sacrifice everything for nation. He leads an inspiring, simple and purposeful life. He possesses the skill of being knowledgeable, punctual and a good orator since he is a role model for society. A pracharak is a full-time worker for the nation. He works mainly according to the needs and demands of the organization, and he goes wherever the organization asks for the work to be done throughout the nation. Hence, he has no personal choice of work or choice of working field – to be absorbed in one action, one mission and one aim. Imagine the lives of these living examples of sacrifice and devotion.

Modi joined RSS when he was only eight years old. His habits of getting up at 5 in the morning and his workaholic nature where he works for eighteen to twenty hours are all the products of his RSS grooming. How to arrive at a consensus after discussing in detail stems from his grooming of attending day-long baithaks (meetings), which discuss the various ideological concepts and how to arrive at a consensus through dialogue and discussion. Many of his ideas on nationalism, humanism, dharma are inspired by mentors like Deendayal Upadhaya, the ideologue of the RSS, who has given the concept of integral humanism.

You cannot be a leader without being a reader. Modi still takes out his time for reading. He has authored many books, which are on different topics of national importance. One of the key habits of a pracharak is valuing time and being punctual. This habit has been one of the most effective and productive habits of Modi. He sleeps for only four hours and even adjusts his sleeping routine according to the time zone if he is travelling abroad to obviate jetlag.

Modi has clarity of thought with respect to purpose, mission and objective of life. Also, he has a deep understanding of the concepts of nationalism, international relations, Hindu rastra, serving society, etc. These ideas are the result of long baithaks in the RSS organization and upbringing. He has also written a complete book on the contributions of pracharaks of Gujarat region and the simple lives of these living legends. Groomed as a pracharak, Modi is always ready to sacrifice everything for the nation. His core ethos is '*pal pal, kan kan*', for the nation speaks how much dedicated he is towards the nation.

Modi is one of the finest orators India has seen after Independence who can connect with the people, knowing their pulse and speaking in their language. He starts the addressing and greetings in the language of people whom he is addressing. The pracharak-Modi is a role model for society and nation, who has sacrificed his personal and familial aspects of life for only single thought with one point dedication. He is working as a full-time worker for the nation. He works according to the needs and requirements of the nation. Hence, he has no personal choice of work or choice of working field. He is absorbed in one action, one mission and one aim.

12

Adrift Opposition Belittling Institutions

Prime Minister Narendra Modi offers prayers at Kedarnath Temple, Uttarakhand

The people in the country accord the highest priority to civility in conduct of political leaders. But a large section of the Opposition parties lacks even the basic courtesy. The utter disregard to the Constitution-mandated protocol by the Opposition leaders is sickening. Such visceral disregard to civility in political life is also suggestive of desperation in the ranks of the Opposition in the face of the ever-rising popularity of Prime Minister Narendra Modi and the Bharatiya Janata Party (BJP).

Sadly, the Aam Aadmi Party, Trinamool Congress, Congress, left parties and others have taken disrespecting the Constitutional positions and protocols as means of politics. Congress egged on the Opposition parties to force the washout of the budget session solely to protect the family interests of the Gandhis. Such coming together to shield dynastic interests is against the interests of democracy.

Telangana Chief Minister K. Chandrashekhar Rao continues to insult the federal structure by skipping the functions of PM Modi. This is against the spirit of the Constitution. His utter disregard for protocol is despite the fact that PM Modi is spearheading development of Telangana.

PM Modi has earned the love of the people, cutting across caste, class, creed and religion on the basis of his hard work for the well-being of the citizens. But the Telangana chief minister has reasons to panic at the sight of PM Modi, which explains why he never fails to skip official protocols during the visit of the prime minister.

But the KCR government sought to silence him by arresting him under a dubious charge. The court promptly freed Bandi Sanjay because there was no merit in the case. It has become a norm in Telangana where the state police would summarily arrest leaders of the BJP. The state government has also faced flak from the Parliamentary privilege committee for one such reckless action against an MP.

It is indeed disturbing that KCR has murdered democracy even though the people had elected him through democratic means. It may be stated that KCR muzzled democracy to give a cover to his clan positioned in all the spheres of the state government. The clan members supervise the looting of the resources of the state while denying the legitimate aspirations of the people, particularly the poor and the weaker sections of society.

The hallmark of a corrupt regime has also been seen in the Indian politics with the emergence of family members in the ruling parties at some places. Telangana is one such example where KCR has brought his entire clan to rule over his party and the state government.

The KCR family members have indulged in enacting political drama after they became certain that the ED would take the case to the logical conclusion. This has clearly set in palpable nervousness in the ranks of the ruling party in Telangana.

KCR has also pressed panic button after becoming convinced that the popularity of PM Modi is only rising in Telangana. This is for the reason that PM Modi in the last nine years has worked for the well-being of small and marginal farmers by protecting their honour with Pradhan Mantri Kisan Samman Nidhi Scheme and weeding out middlemen in procurement of food grains and distribution of urea.

KCR is in panic in the face of increasing unpopularity of his government. He is now resorting to undemocratic and repressive measures to stifle the voice of the BJP. But he is harbouring misplaced notions. The people of the country have always thrown such people who have shown anti-democratic mindsets. KCR may have forgotten, but even the most repressive of the regimes have been thrown out by the people for failing to respect democratic norms.

The BJP would be unwavering in its struggle for the legitimate rights of the people in Telangana. The people in Telangana are fed up with the KCR and his family rule. The BJP leadership is committed to protecting the interests of the people of Telangana, and democracy will be fully restored in the state soon.

Late Rajiv Gandhi was the leader of the Opposition in the Lok Sabha in 1990, when the then Prime Minister Vishwanath Pratap Singh took the historic decision to implement the Mandal Commission Report to give effect of reservation to other backward castes (OBCs) to the extent of 27 per cent. Six years before Rajiv Gandhi had led Congress to win 404 seats with over 49 per cent vote share.

The Mandal Commission Report was a turnaround for Indian politics, as Rajiv Gandhi stood in the Lok Sabha to oppose its implementation. The Bharatiya Janata Party leaders Atal Bihari Vajpayee and L.K. Advani had welcomed the decision of the V.P. Singh government, stating that the time had come to recognize the legitimate demands of the OBCs in the country.

The stand of Rajiv Gandhi was almost unilateral, as records of those times show that the OBC leaders within the Congress were appalled at the decision of their leaders. The Congress leaders were shocked that Rajiv Gandhi was disconnected from the masses. He was not ready for the march of social justice.

Within a few years, Congress was reduced to a party with the best tally of about 200 Lok Sabha seats, even when the party came to power in alliance with other political parties. With the strength of 404 Lok Sabha seats,

Congress' fortune was cut by half in the Lok Sabha, solely for its anti-OBC mindset. The space vacated by Congress was occupied by the regional parties. They mushroomed all across the country. Political parties espousing the cause of the OBCs came up in Haryana, Uttar Pradesh, Andhra Pradesh and elsewhere. They ate into the vote base of Congress. Even after three decades, Congress has mostly lost its vote base in states where the OBC identity-based regional parties cropped up.

The BJP was clear from the very beginning that the OBC deserved social justice, and the party's leadership was steadfast in their support. The BJP's support to the OBC was also manifested in a strong leadership of the party from the backward castes. They were at the forefront of the party workers in several states. They also took the leadership of the party and even became chief ministers.

The journey of Congress and the BJP is in sharp contrast. Congress has been in a steep political fall since 1990s. The BJP has rapidly risen in its political stock since the 1990s. The Congress base shrank. The BJP vote base expanded. Congress kept hitting lower and lower in its Lok Sabha tally. The BJP tally in the Lok Sabha kept rising.

In the 1989 Lok Sabha elections, Congress had won 197 seats. The BJP had won 85 Lok Sabha seats in the same election. Three decades later, the BJP won 303 Lok Sabha seats in the 2019 Lok Sabha elections. Congress for the second time in a row could not win enough seats to gain the status of the leader of the Opposition in the Lok Sabha. The people of the country punished Congress for its anti-OBC bias in the last three decades.

Rahul Gandhi repeated the same mistake that his father had committed in the Lok Sabha in 1990. There is not a single independent voice in the country that didn't admonish him for his 2019 election speech in Kolar, Karnataka, in which he asked, 'Why all thieves have the Modi surname?' This was an outrageous statement by a person who was president of Congress. He had been a member of the Lok Sabha multiple times. He is also fifty-two years old. He couldn't have made such a scandalous and outrageous statement to question the integrity of the OBC community.

Worse is the fact that there is no remorse on the part of Rahul Gandhi. He had occasions to express remorse and apologize in the Surat Court. But he chose not to apologize. It's beyond understanding that a number of lawyers who hold senior positions in the Congress would not have gauged the consequences of Rahul Gandhi not apologizing for his defamatory statement.

Also, there had been a number of precedents in which senior political leaders escaped the judicial fury by apologizing in the court. Delhi chief minister Arvind Kejriwal had also levelled baseless allegations to defame late Arun Jaitley and Union Minister Nitin Gadkari. Both forgave him after he apologized for his mistakes. But here, Rahul Gandhi doesn't want to own up to his mistake. Instead, he has chosen to enact political stunts in the name of his conviction by the court in criminal defamation case and the subsequent automatic disqualification from the membership of the Lok Sabha, which was in accordance with the Supreme Court ruling of 2013.

Rajiv Gandhi's anti-OBC stand had cut Congress' strength by half. Rahul Gandhi's stand against the OBC will also bring similar wrath, and the Opposition party, given its current strength, may find itself among the regional parties sitting in one corner of the Lok Sabha with only a handful members after the 2024 general elections.

History reveals the truth for the people despite all attempts to manufacture lies. Rahul Gandhi's insult to the OBC community should not surprise anyone. People with long-term memory know that this has been done before. It's just in the DNA of Congress to insult the OBC community. Even his father, Rajiv Gandhi, as leader of the Opposition in the Lok Sabha in 1990, opposed Vishwanath Pratap Singh, the then prime minister, who announced the implementation of the Mandal Commission report, the epochal moment that sought to give effect to reservation to other backward castes (OBCs) to the extent of 27 per cent. That was a decade of Congress heydays, with the party having won 404 Lok Sabha seats in 1984 with over 49 per cent vote share. Rajiv Gandhi stood in the Lok Sabha to oppose the implementation of the OBC reservation.

13

Narendra Modi: India's Foremost Cultural Ambassador

Prime Minister Narendra Modi unveiling a bust of Mahatma Gandhi in Hiroshima, Japan

Prime Minister Narendra Modi has been India's foremost cultural ambassador for the outside world. Modi has also been a change agent for the cultural renaissance in India. Under his careful watch, India rediscovered its cultural glory. From the grand construction of the Ram Temple at Ayodhya to the redevelopment of the Vishwanath Temple in Varanasi, from the grand makeover of the Mahakal Temple in Ujjain to bringing back stolen antique wealth of

India, Modi steered emotional connection of the people at the centre stage of his state craft.

The Indian civilization, which is also known as Sanatan Parmpara, is among the oldest civilizations in the world. Pauranic legends say the oldest city of the universe is Varanasi, also known as Banaras or Kashi. Every Hindu aspires to go on a pilgrimage to Kashi at least once in his lifetime and also wishes to breathe his last there.

It is practically the spiritual capital of India and is one among the Saptpuris, one among twelve Jyotirlingas, one of the fifty-two Shakti Peethas and one among the Tristhalis. Kashi is said to have been founded on the Trident of Lord Shiva and anyone who dies here gets Moksha.The main deity is known by the names Shri Vishwanath and Vishweshwara, literally meaning 'Lord of the Universe'.Varanasi was called Kashi in ancient times, and hence the temple is popularly called Kashi Vishwanath Temple. Kashi, in fact, is the land of Lord Shiva.

Located on the banks of the river Ganga, this city has attracted seers and seekers, tourists and wanderers alike, from time immemorial. It is as a tribute to the holy city that Prime Minister Narendra Modi conceived the Kashi Vishwanath Corridor Project and laid its foundation stone in March 2019.

As an ardent devotee of Lord Shiva and the Indian culture, the prime minister took upon himself the near-impossible task of reviving the lost glory of this divine city. In fact, it is not just the beautification and cleanliness of the city; the project is aimed at the cultural revival of India's rich heritage and traditions represented by temple cities like this.

Features of the Kashi Vishwanath Corridor Project

Kashi is known for two things-temples and ghats. The main aim of the project was to connect these two things – the Kashi Vishwanath Temple and the river Ganga. The project connects the temple with the ghats with a paved walkway. Area-wise, it is one of the biggest temple corridor projects in India. The corridor is built over 5.5 lakh square feet. The project aims to increase the total area of the temple to around 50,000 square meters. The people of Kashi were made a part of this project, and they were urged to give their land for the project. Over 300 buildings adjoining the temple were purchased to create the space for the project. They were given the market value of their properties.

The main temple was earlier surrounded by buildings on three sides; the corridor has decongested the temple complex. The construction and dig-up have led to the recovery of at least forty ancient temples. There is no tinkering or tampering with the original structure of the Kashi Vishwanath Temple. Without compromising the originality of the ancient structure, the beauty, splendour and magnificence of Kashi have been enhanced. The project aims at making this corridor a centre for religious-cultural tourism. The work includes the construction of Temple Chowk, Varanasi city gallery, multipurpose auditoriums, halls, museum, devotee facilitation centre, public convenience, salvation home, Godowlia gate, Bhogshala, shelter for priests and sevadars, spiritual book space, etc.

The other facilities include an over 7,000-square-metre temple platform for meditation for 10,000 people, seven grand entrance gates, a cafeteria, a food court, a Vedic and spiritual library, a virtual gallery. A special sky beam light system is also installed along the corridor. To protect the ecology and environment, about 70 per cent of the 5.50 lakh sq. ft area of the project is kept open for the green cover. Nearly ₹1,000 crore has been spent on the entire project, which includes ₹70 crore on the rehabilitation of people living in the redeveloped area.

To make it a true religious-cultural event, the inauguration would see the presence of the main acharya's of the twelve Jyotirlingas, with water from all major rivers of the country being brought in for the abhishek of the main deity Baba Vishwanath (Lord Shiva). Modi has also been an ardent follower of Kedarnath. Under his watch, the redevelopment of the Kedarnath Temple was carried out at great speed and scale. His government also gave a tremendous push to the infrastructure development for the Char Dham yatra, which is a major boost for the religious tourism in Uttarakhand.

India is primarily a religious-spiritual civilization and country. It will boost not only domestic tourism but will also attract worldwide spiritual tourism, which is India's strong point. The revival of our cultural heritage like this will not only enhance tourism potential and tourist economy but will also help in the spread of Indian culture in a better way.

Modi deputed his former aide, Nripendra Mishra, former principal secretary in Prime Minister's Office, to oversee the construction of the Ram Temple at Ayodhya.

The scale of the construction is aimed at establishing Ayodhya at the heart of the Indian cultural renaissance. The people's participation in the construction of the temple has been phenomenal.

Modi also brought the Indian culture to the forefront during the G20 Leaders' Summit in New Delhi. Various exhibitions were set up at Bharat Mandapam to showcase India's cultural heritage, handicrafts, technological prowess and innovation. These exhibitions offered a multitude of unique experiences for visitors.

Modi received the heads of the states ahead of the G20 Leaders' Summit at Bharat Mandapam with the portrait of the Konark Wheel in the background. Konark Wheel was built during the 13th century under the reign of King Narasimhadeva I, and it remains India's foremost cultural wealth, attracting visitors from all around the world. The wheel with twenty-four spokes is also adapted into India's national flag and embodies India's ancient wisdom, advanced civilization and architectural excellence. The rotating motion of the Konark Wheel symbolizes time, Kalachakra as well as progress and continuous change. It serves as a powerful symbol of the wheel of democracy that reflects the resilience of democratic ideals and commitment to progress in society. It also represents dharma, duty and principles of governance. The Konark Wheel was set out in the background of the reception for the heads of the states ahead of the G20 Leaders' Summit symbolizing that they have a foremost duty to the well-being of global humanity and that no narrow considerations should come in dedicating all efforts for the betterment of humanity.

Additionally, the ruins of Nalanda Mahavira were also put as the backdrop at the G20 Leaders' Summit at Bharat Mandapam to send a powerful message on principles of governance from the rich ancient Indian heritage. In operation between 5th century and 12th century, legacy of Nalanda Mahavira goes back to Buddha's and Mahavira's eras reflecting ancient India's advancement towards disseminating knowledge and wisdom. Its embrace of diversity, meritocracy, freedom of thought, collective governance, autonomy and knowledge sharing all align with the core principles of democracy.

Reputed as one of the earliest international universities in the world, Nalanda is a living testament to the enduring spirit of India's advanced educational pursuit and its commitment to build a harmonious world community, aligning with India's G20 presidency theme Vasudhaiva Kutumbakam.

Also, Modi has been instrumental in bringing back the stolen cultural wealth of India from all parts of the world. More than 231 stolen antiques had been brought back to India in the first nine years after Prime Minister Narendra Modi took over as the head of the government. This is in contrast to the fact that till 2014, for almost seventy years since Independence, just about thirteen invaluable heritage antiques of Indian origin were brought back from abroad by previous governments.

A total of 231 were brought back after 2014, with the number now going up to 244 antiques.[1] The process of bringing more of such antiquities has been continuing on fast track. In the first nine years with Modi at the helm, several unique new initiatives had been undertaken, one of which was setting up of science museums across the country and a beginning had been made by setting up science museums in aspirational districts.

Bharat Mandapam showcased 'Culture Corridor G20 Digital Museum'. The culture corridor represented and celebrated the shared heritage of G20 members and invitee countries. It incorporated iconic and notable cultural objects and heritage of the G20 members and nine invitee countries. This Culture Corridor was meant to serve as a powerful platform for promoting understanding and appreciation of diverse cultural expressions, for knowledge sharing, inclusivity and equality, and for fostering a sense of shared identity.

A 'Crafts Bazaar' was set up at Bharat Mandapam to showcase handicraft products from different parts of India with a special focus on 'One District One Product' and GI-tagged items. It offered G20 delegates the unique opportunity to purchase locally sourced products. Around thirty states and UTs as well as central agencies like Khadi Village and Industries Commission, Tribal Co-operative Marketing Development Federation of India (TRIFED), etc., participated in the Crafts Bazaar. To showcase the skills and exquisite workmanship of artisans, special live demonstrations by master craftsmen were also held.

Modi in his several speeches at the United Nations quoted the greatest Tamil poet Thiruvalluvar. He hailed the greatness of Tamil language from the international stage. Modi has been the foremost cultural ambassador for India as he hosted the world leaders at venues of India's rich heritage, including Chinese president Xi Jinping at

Mammalpuram in Tamil Nadu. He also hosted world leaders in Varanasi.

During his foreign visits, Modi offers gifts to heads of the states which give glimpses into India's rich cultural heritage. His gifts to the world leaders have shown Modi's commitment to promoting the rich cultural heritage of each region of India. Also, Modi has special emotional connections with the skills of the artisans. His gifts to the world leaders are often the works of artisans from all parts of India.

14

Modi and Mahatma: Too Many Parallels

Prime Minister Narendra Modi celebrates the 553rd birth anniversary of Guru Nanakdev Ji in New Delhi

The holy land of India has been incarnating great human beings from time to time. In the 20th century, one such great human being was Mohan Das Karamchand Gandhi, born on 2 October 1869 at Porbandar (Gujarat). Mahatma Gandhi not only fought for the freedom of the country, but even after independence, he had dreamt of a strong India.

Unfortunately, the Congress party, which had been doing politics riding on his pious name, vehemently ignored his policies and dreams. Prime Minister Narendra Modi took the pledge to make Bapu's dreams come true and also acted to make his dreams a reality. While fighting for the freedom struggle, Mahatma Gandhi converted the freedom struggle into a mass movement for the first time in the history of the country.

By doing the same, he made the whole world realize the power of the people of India. Similarly, Prime Minister Narendra Modi also directly linked and dedicated the important decisions of his government to the benefit of a large number of people. He also aimed to make every Indian's dream a reality. The most favourite line of the father of the nation Mahatma Gandhi was '*vaishnav jan to tene kahiye, peer parai jaane re*'.

By following the same path, Prime Minister Narendra Modi understood the plight of the poor after six decades of Independence and opened all the ways and resources of the country to remove their suffering. In every decision, programmes and schemes of the Modi government, each and every person of the country has been taken into account and furthering their welfare remains the priority of the present Modi government. Mahatma Gandhi was a custodian of peace and non-violence. To keep these two intact, Prime Minister Modi is leaving no stone unturned to take India on the path of *viswaguru* (world leader) with his efficiency and contemplation by attacking and eliminating the elements causing any hindrance in the progress of the country.

He gave the message to the whole world that India is the land of Buddha and not of war. And the era in which we are living is not an era of war. The message has been conveyed and sent across the world. Narendra Modi's endeavour to fight against terrorism, extremism and hatred has even sent shock waves to the isolated anti-India groups, which are always endearing to project India as violent and aggressive. These groups keep on reorganizing and mobilizing such elements against India as they never want to see a strong India.

Mahatma Gandhi considered cleanliness very important and was of the view that cleanliness could lead to freedom from poverty and disease in the country. When Narendra Modi became the prime minister of the country, he initiated the *Swachh Bharat Abhiyan* (clean India drive). He made this campaign a nation-wide mass movement. From the streets of the village to the metropolitan cities, from old to young, every citizen joined this campaign.

In furtherance of this campaign, the Modi government constructed and dedicated 11 crore toilets for the people. This campaign was started on 2 October 2014 on the birthday of Mahatma Gandhi. The Father of the Nation freed the country from the clutches of slavery, but his dream of 'Clean India' was not fulfilled. Mahatma Gandhi gave a top-notch message to the nation by inspiring people around him to maintain cleanliness.

When Prime Minister Narendra Modi took the initiative to fulfil this dream of Bapu, it was for the first time that such a large movement involving so many people was witnessed in India. The philosophy of

Swachh Bharat Abhiyan, started during the first term of PM Modi, was based on the life principles of Mahatma Gandhi. The prime minister's appeal to all the citizens of India to join it for the successful implementation of Swachh Bharat Abhiyan turned it into a mass movement.

Under this campaign, the prime minister was able to interlink the inspirational ideas of cleanliness with self-respect and dignity, and as a result, the dream of an open-defecation free country was possible, which is no less than a revolution in itself. Gandhi laid emphasis on economic independence and self-reliance. The plan for the use of Khadi for the fulfilment of 'Gram Swaraj', self-government, self-reliance and economic independence was based on Gandhi's philosophy. Though the country became politically independent in 1947, economic independence remained a dream for the poor.

Economic freedom and self-reliance are the pillars on which the upliftment of the poor can be done. In the 1970s, slogans of '*gareebi hatao*' (remove poverty) were raised in the country, but no effective scheme or programme was initiated by the then governments to remove it. The policies of the government were confined just to slogans and not to work on ground. Aatmanirbhar Bharat (self-reliant India) campaign started by Prime Minister Narendra Modi is committed to freeing the poor from the clutches of poverty and slavery to make them the masters of their own destiny.

The policies related to the farmers' welfare and essential commodities initiated by the Modi government have taken a concrete step towards providing economic freedom and better economical options to the farmers.

The prime minister is trying in a systematic way to turn his dream of a self-reliant India (Aatmanirbhar Bharat) into a reality. He first projected the principles of self-reliance and then gave them a huge financial package for implementation. Even before the Modi government, many governments have taken inspiration from the principles of Gandhi's life and thoughts, but no prime minister has made any effort to turn the dream of Gandhi into reality. Let us take the example of Khadi, which remained largely neglected.

Khadi was promoted at a large scale during the Modi government. Today, Khadi has become popular not only in India but also abroad. The business of Khadi has increased under the 'Vocal for Local' campaign, started by the Modi government. On 2 October the country celebrates the birth anniversary of Mahatma Gandhi as well as of the former prime minister Lal Bahadur Shastri.

Earlier, Atalji added 'Jai Vigyan' to Shastri ji's 'Jai Jawan Jai Kisan' slogan and now, in view of the policies of the last eight years of the Modi government and the recent laws made, Modi added 'Jai Anusandhan' (research) this year.

With Convenient Action-Continuity for Change, 'green crusader' Modi has become the second politician in the world, after the former US vice-president Al Gore, to pen a book on climate change. Modi is an environmentally sound statesman. As per Indian traditions and ethos, earth is revered as mother. We call it *Dhar Mata* who gives us food to sustain, space to live, air to breathe and bounty of resources to enjoy. This ethos is ingrained in the culture of India and assimilated so well in our day-to-day lives.

One of the duties of the king as per *Arthashastra* is to save the natural resources and natural assets of the nation. World over, you will find very few politicians who, besides politics, are also working as environmental statesmen. India in this sense is fortunate enough to be headed by a statesman who is an environmental crusader besides being an environmentalist in the true sense. As a child, Modi has lived and grown up in an ambience which venerates the environment and in which the mother earth and its resources like trees, rivers, flora and fauna are worshipped. As a pracharak in RSS, he lived a life of minimalism where you survive only with your very basic material needs. This has had a profound impact on his views on environment and earth. Even as the CM of Gujarat, he has been a crusader of saving the environment.

He has written a book *Convenient Action-Community for Change* which underlines his environmental ethos. The views of Modi on environment resonate with the Indian ethos which has evolved over many centuries. Everything on the planet is composed of five elements – *panch tatva*, i.e., air, water, space, earth and fire. So saving these five elements is saving the environment. Human being is an extension of the planet. For him, Earth is the giver and sustainer of life, hence is hailed as Mother Earth.

The concept of 'Vasudhev Katumbkam' (whole universe is family) is the basis of this cultural ethos where we live in cooperation and harmony not only with the fellow human beings but with all the other creatures like animal, birds and plants. Man and nature have a complementary relationship, which is embodied in the ancient Vedic literature. As per it, respect for nature is an integral part of our culture and comes naturally to us. Further, as per the Vedic literature, it is not that environment has failed us, rather we have failed the environment.

Living sustainably and ensuring a lifestyle which not only sustains us but also sustains the future generation is his core philosophy. He has given a new meaning to the concept of 'Trusteeship', which means that we are not the owners of the natural resources but just trustees of these resources which belong to future generations. So it is our moral duty to protect these resources. For this, as human beings, we have to change our habits and develop habits which are in conformity with the nature. He calls upon us to bring small changes in our day-to-day lives. He suggests climate ethics which are environment-friendly habits and which envisage a sustainable future for our planet, as the basis of living as part of nature.

To quote him 'For me, this (saving environment) is a moral issue. You don't have a right to exploit what belongs to future generations. We are only allowed to milk the earth, not to kill it.' From climate ethics, he has moved to climate justice, emphasizing sensitivity towards nature and natural resources and keeping in mind the interests of the poor and downtrodden. He has been consistently urging the entire community of world leaders to take actionable steps for dealing with climate change without any delay. He speaks about green economy when he says that we have to move towards 'zero defect and zero effect', i.e., zero defects in production with no adverse effect on environment.

Economy and ecology are mutually inclusive. One cannot grow without the growth of other. Our economy should be so developed that it does not harm the environment. With these views in background, the prime minister has tried to put in practice each of his ideas as a part of policies of his government.

Launched on 2 October 2014 at Raj Ghat, New Delhi, Swachch Bharat Abhiyan is India's biggest cleanliness drive ever. To make it a mass movement, he even nominated nine prominent public figures from the country to support and encourage the initiative which will cover as many as 4,041 towns and aim at cleaning streets, roads and infrastructure. 'Namami Gange' project aim at a clean Ganga which is our most revered and important water body.

For this a total of ₹20,000 crore to conserve and rejuvenate the river was allocated by involving the people living on the banks of the river and helping them attain sustainable livelihoods and feel the impact first-hand. Focusing on bringing down soaring pollution levels in the country, Prime Minister Narendra Modi launched India's first national air quality index (NAQI) in April 2015. IIT Kanpur will house the main server of the NAQI which will monitor air quality levels in ten cities throughout the country. For water conservation, the states of India are to ensure that 50 per cent of the work taken up by MNREGA should be for the improvement of water conservation. This includes construction of check dams and desilting of water bodies.

Narendra Modi himself asked farmers across the country to adopt modern ways of conserving water.

He gave the mantra '*pehle shauchalaya, phir devalaya*' (first toilets, then temples). He is working relentlessly to ensure that affordable sanitation reaches the people who need it. Saving power by using LED lights and providing electricity to each household, thereby reducing dependence on biodegradable resources, is a positive step in this direction.

He is stressing on local technology and his campaign of Vocal for Local aims at reducing the carbon footprints.

International Approach

When Modi was the CM of Gujarat, Hollywood action-movie star Arnold Schwarzenegger praised his 'actions' as Gujarat chief minister to achieve sustainable development goals. Under him, India and France formed the one of its kind International Solar Alliance for developing solar energy. He is the person who brought into focus the concept of renewable energy. To highlight the significance of flora and fauna, he has appeared in a popular Discovery channel show *Man vs. Wild* with Bear Grylls. India is one of the few countries to have initiated the ban on single-use plastic. He has been felicitated with 'Champion of the Earth' award by United Nations Environment Programme (UNEP) and CERAWeek Global Energy and Environment Leadership Award. India is emerging as a champion of sustainable development and a crusader of global warming under him.

It is said that we should mind our thoughts, since thoughts become actions; we should watch our actions, since actions become habits and we should watch our habits since habits become our character; and it is the character which decides our destiny. As per Socrates, 90 per cent of what we think and act is habit. So excellence is not a singular act but a way of life. Successful people are successful because they have successful habits. First, we make habits then habits make us. We are what our habits are. In his book *The 7 Habits of Highly Effective People*, Stephen R. Covey speaks of the habits of highly effective people, which are based on timeless principles of fairness, integrity, honesty and human dignity.

In his seminal work, James Clear speaks of atomic habits of success followed by successful people. These are habits which put successful people at the top. Let us learn the successful and highly effective habits of one of the most successful statesmen in the world. Modi is proactive instead of reactive. Stephen R. Covey has given this as the basis of all the other habits. It means in every situation you are in charge. Instead of reacting to the situation, you can do something to change the situation. Action replaces reaction. This is one of the traits of Modi that instead of 'reacting' to any situation, he takes on responsibility to change the situation. He is an action-oriented man who believes in karma, irrespective of the results. Action for the sake of action is his core philosophy.

He focuses and acts on what he can change and influence instead of what he can't. Instead of blaming others, he takes upon himself and solves that situation himself. This makes him a super proactive and action-oriented person. As per him, we are the product of our choices. It also implies that he does all of his daily work on his own instead of depending on others. Imagine that he himself picked the broom and started cleaning the road to launch the largest cleanliness drive, Swachh Bharat Mission on 2 October. You can see him holding his own umbrella instead of asking his security personnel to do so for him.

Clarity of Goal and Plan

One of the habits of successful people is that they have a clear goal and a definite plan to fulfil their mission. They have a life plan, decade plan, yearly plan, monthly plan and even daily plan. As per one study, ten minutes of planning saves 1/6 time in execution of the plan. Modi starts his day by planning the day in detail. It includes what is to be done for the day. More importantly, it is what is to be done first and in priority. So one of the key lessons is to plan and prioritize the day and work. It gives focus on what is important and what is to come first. It saves you from digressing and off-tracking from the main and important issues.

Getting Up Early and Doing Yoga

One of the habits of successful corporate leaders is getting up early in the morning. Modi gets up at 4 a.m. in the morning, and this routine has been followed since he was in public life. After waking up, walking, yoga, Surya Namaskar and meditation are his first things which keep his body and mind in highly effective and efficient mode. He is conscious of his food, as food is the energy which keeps you going. There are people who live for food and there are people who eat to live. Modi belongs to the latter category as for him eating is meant as pure, simple and healthy food so as to be your best version.

Work is Worship

Successful people have a mantra. For them, work is worship. It is not only a source of official dues but a way of expressing your personality. For Modi, his work is a way to express his creativity and a divine duty which he performs with full dedication and devotion. He is a true *karamyogi* who works for the sake of work and follows the ethics of Karma Yoga in which you work for the pleasure of work without attaching yourself to the results or rewards of the work you have done. Even at the age of seventy-one, he works for twenty hours and sleeps only for four hours, and this routine has been followed by him since long. Even during travelling, he spends his time working. Leaders are readers: one of the traits of a successful person is that they are avid readers. You are the average of five persons whom you spent your time with. Therefore, a successful person always reads so as to learn from the life experiences of the others. Modi is not only a great reader but also an author. As a young boy in Vadnagar, he frequented the local library regularly. His keen areas of interest are cultural heritage, ancient history and political science.

Reading books increases motivation, energy and life balance by making time for renewing activities. It helps with what is called 'sharpen the saw', another habit mentioned by Stephen Covey.

Communicate

Successful people communicate effectively both within and outside. What you communicate with yourself is what you become, what you communicate with others becomes your image. To remain positive, one has to communicate positive and noble thoughts to himself. The internal communication of Modi is always internal motivation, working for the nation, using each neuron in his body and each moment of his life in the service (*kan kan, pal pal*) of the people and the nation. Also, being a versatile orator, he communicates with others in a way which touches them emotionally and inspires them. Success is not a matter of chance; it is a matter of 'choice'. If we want to be successful, we have to follow the path followed by successful people.

Global leader is defined as a leader who leads people of the world across various regions, cultures and time zones. In international relationship and theory, a never-ending debate goes on as to who influences diplomacy: Is it the influence of the nation or is it the influence of the leader of the nation? In diplomatic jargon, 'global leader' is a term used in two senses: a person-specific global leader is the one who has influence over world affairs far greater than his country's and a country-specific global leader is the national leader who wields influence in the world because he represents a powerful country.

While person-specific global leaders are leaders owing to their personal attributes like charisma and their crusade for some noble cause; the nation-specific global leaders drive their influence on account of the power and influence of their country, be it power of geo-economics, geo-politics or geo-strategic. There have been very rare occasions in world history when both personal-specific and global-specific leadership merge and work in tandem.

It depends upon many factors like the understanding and interests of the world affairs of the national leader, his pro-activity in diplomacy, his charisma, his views on common global problems and solutions, his personal relationships with the leaders of other countries, so and so forth. To take a middle path, a healthy combination of diplomacy as well as personal leadership can be used to influence the international relationship in favour of national interest.

Modi and Foreign Policy

We find a perceptible change in Indian foreign policy over the past few years, which is a combination of dynamic leadership riding on brewing superpower. It is driven by personal diplomacy with the ultimate aim of maximizing the national interest of India through the use of diplomacy. Ever since Modi took over as PM, India's diplomacy has emerged as one of the core areas of his leadership.

The key ethos of his foreign policy can be enumerated as under: (a) Global leader-based diplomacy, which is the combination of personality and national power; (b) Pro-active diplomacy with its different aspects of economic diplomacy, cultural diplomacy, defence diplomacy, which is used with the only aim of enhancing the Indian national interest; (c) Use of geo-politics to strengthen India's economy.

There is a 180-degree shift in India's foreign policy under Modi. He is the most followed statesman of the world be it on Twitter or on any other social media platform. He has domestic support from all quarters of the population. There is proactive diplomacy on all the issues. As the leader of the nation, he believes in touring the whole world and addressing India's concerns and national interests.

He is also rewiring and rebranding Brand-India from a soft state to a nation with power, which can influence the world's affairs in a positive manner. He is using India diaspora to the maximum advantage of India's national interests. He is the leader who enjoys maximum support and following by India diaspora. Wherever he goes, he meets the non-resident Indians (NRI) or persons of Indian origin (PIO) so as to re-attach them with India at a new level. The success of these events can be gauged from successful and impactful conducting of the Howdy Modi event.

The other perceptible thing which he has done is making India a superpower in the field of defence. Our defence basket is now expanded to multi-players and multi-groups and from various countries, thereby ending India's reliance on a few countries. With his extensive tours and meetings with the leaders of the world, he has developed a personal-level rapport with many of the leaders, which is helping India further its point of view on many issues and debunking many stereotypes. He is also projecting India's culture through cultural diplomacy.

None could imagine that the world will celebrate India's gift to the world in the form of yoga on

International Yoga Day. It has been done following hectic cultural diplomacy. The way Modi brought to front the new challenging issues of religious extremism, global terrorism, environmental concerns highlights the fact that India is influencing and shaping the world's events on global issues facing the entire humanity. True to its ethos of 'Vasudhev Kutumbkam', India has helped the world with Vaccine-Maitri diplomacy. India has shown the path to the world as how to move ahead in vaccination with a record of 2.26 crore vaccinations in a day.[1] India is now emerging as a global leader in the true sense of leadership.

15

Narendra Modi: A True Punjabi with Love for the Northeast

Prime Minister Narendra Modi meets a Sikh delegation at 7 Lok Kalyan Marg

Punjab, the breadbasket of the country, has given many politicians and leaders, including a prime minister and a president, to India. Whereas the reign of President Zail Singh saw the infamous attack on the Golden Temple under the regime of the Congress government in 1984, the reign of Manmohan Singh, who served as prime minister twice, did not see any special favour to Punjab though he claimed to be a hardcore Punjabi. His tenure was marked by tensions and conflicts between the Centre and Punjab.

However, since 2014 a visible change can be seen in Punjab and Punjabis, be it in the policies of the Centre or the personal touch for the sentiments of the Punjabis or healing the long-term pains and issues of the Punjabis. It is said that state policy is influenced much by the perception of the person who is at the helm of affairs. Modi has a special love, affection and tilt towards Punjab, Punjabis and Punjabiat.

He has always praised the contribution made by the Punjabis in nation-making, particularly its valiant Sikh community. In his encouraging speech in the Parliament, he has eulogized that India can never repay the debts of the Sikhs and the sacrifice made by this community in its history and every Indian is proud of the Sikhs (8 February 2021). His love and special relationship with Punjabis and Sikhs took root in his days as his party's point man in Punjab, where he worked at close quarters with Sikh leaders and stalwarts such as Parkash Singh Badal and many others. How much love and respect he has for Punjab and Sikhs can be gauged from the fact that he has hailed this stalwart leader of Punjab as the Nelson Mandela of India.

Who could forget the picture of Narendra Modi publicly touching the feet of Badal out of his sheer respect for his age and contribution to society and nation-making before the swearing in of the NDA government. This respect and love are not only reflected in the actions, speeches and narratives of the prime minister but also in the policies followed by the Modi government with respect to Punjabis, and particularly Sikhs. The long-standing demand of Punjabis was justice for the Sikhs who were massacred in 1984 in various parts of India following a state-sponsored, party-led Sikh killings. The epicentre of this massacre was Delhi where Congress leaders led the mob and killed our innocent Punjabi brethren in one of the most shameful and cowardly attacks on Punjabis since 1947. The Modi government formed a Special Investigative Team (SIT) to bring to justice the perpetrators of this heinous crime and with regular and responsible follow-up of legal process. The main accused, Sajjan Kumar, who was one of the kingpins of the massacre and the key leader of Congress, is behind the bar and there are many more others to follow.

Justice is delivered after thirty-five years that too when the whole entrenched system was there to protect the accused. What the eight successive governments could not do and the sufferer had lost all hopes, justice was not only seen to be delivered but was actually delivered. Also, compensation for the aggrieved families was sanctioned only after the personal monitoring of Modi under his government. Close to 50,000 Punjabis, particularly Sikhs, who were living the life of wanderers and without any statehood following political asylum during the black days, were given passports by his government. Even the dreaded blacklist created by the earlier regimes to witch-hunt the youth was done away with by bringing the blacklisted Punjabis into the mainstream. Modi Ji has special respect for the Sikh Gurus and Sikh Panth.

One of the historic steps towards Punjabi and Punjabiat was the opening of the Kartarpur Corridor by the personal efforts of Narendra Modi. Not only Kartarpur Corridor was opened but the whole project of Kartarpur Corridor was given a world-class outlook. How Punjabis could forget the image of Modi taking Langar with other dignitaries on the occasion of opening ceremony of Shri Kartarpur Sahib. The 550th birth anniversary of Guru Nanak Dev Ji was celebrated as an international event, wherein it was celebrated in all the offices of Government of India in whole of the world. Also, Modi introduced a commemorative coin of ₹350 to mark 350th birth anniversary of our 10th Guru Gobind Singh Ji at his birthplace in Patna. Recently, paying rich tributes to the tenth Sikh Guru on the occasion of Parkash Purab of Sri Guru Gobind Singh Ji and befitting tribute to the courage of the Sahibzades and their quest for justice, 26 December is marked as 'Veer Baal Diwas', which will be celebrated as such henceforth by this Punjabi at heart, Modi. We must not forget the humility with which he withdrew the farm laws and the occasion on which he withdrew clearly spoke of the love he has for Punjabis and the Sikhs. Probably, we have a prime minister who is the most Punjabi in his heart!

The golden age of freedom (Azaadi ka Amrit Mahotsav) is going on. It is not a matter of misfortune that after Independence, the Congress governments in India did not make any concrete ground efforts for the economic development of the Northeast, nor did they work to integrate the citizens there into the mainstream of development. Because of this, the feeling of natural affinity towards this part in the rest of the country could not be formed in that way.

The BJP-led NDA government under the leadership of Atal Bihari Vajpayee took the initiative of development in the Northeast for the first time and formed a separate ministry for it, but after that there was no special effort for the development of the Northeast in the ten years of the UPA government of the Congress. After Prime Minister Narendra Modi assumed office in 2014, a new story of all-round development of Northeast India has been written. Earlier, the states of Northeast used to struggle with the problems of insurgency, infiltration, bandh, blockade, drug smuggling, corruption and caste tension, but Prime Minister Narendra Modi gave the entire Northeast the form of *Ashtalakshmi* and gave it development, connectivity, infrastructure development. It has become a major hub of IT, industrial development, sports, investment and organic farming. Narendra Modi focused on the balanced and rapid development of every state of the country so that the country could become self-reliant. Prime Minister Narendra Modi's 'Act East' policy instead of 'Look East' policy has seen unprecedented changes in the Ashtalakshmi states of the Northeast in the last nine years.

After becoming the prime minister, Narendra Modi alone has visited the Northeast more times than all the prime ministers have visited the northeastern states after the Independence of the country. Due to this, development is happening at a fast pace here. The result of this change in Delhi's thinking about the Northeast is that the Northeast is now becoming the gateway to India's development. The mantras 'Vocal for Local' and 'Local for Global' have given pace to this development. For a long time, there was a belief in the country that if there is development in the border area, then the enemy will be benefited. Due to this pessimistic attitude and lack of political will, connectivity could not improve in all the border areas of the country including the Northeast. Now Prime Minister Narendra Modi has emphasized the development of Highway, Inland Waterway, Railway and Airway (HIRA).

This has bridged the heartland gap between the northeastern states, the rest of India and Delhi. In December 2022, Prime Minister Modi visited the Northeast and laid the foundation of development projects worth thousands of crores. In the last nine years, the Modi government has shown 'red cards' to many obstacles related to the development of Meghalaya. Work is going on fast to connect all the capitals of Northeast including Shillong with rail service. In Meghalaya, air service is running on sixteen routes under the UDAN scheme. Farmers in Meghalaya and the Northeast are also benefiting from better air connectivity. With the Krishi Udaan scheme of the Central government, fruits and vegetables here are easily reaching the markets of the country and abroad. In the last nine years, ₹5,000 crore has been spent on the construction of the national highway in Meghalaya. The number of rural roads built in the last nine years under the Pradhan Mantri Sadak Yojana in Meghalaya is seven times more than what was built in the previous twenty years.

Digital connectivity is creating new opportunities for the youth power of the Northeast. Compared to 2014, optical fibre coverage in the Northeast has increased by almost four times. In Meghalaya, this increase is more than five times. Thousands of mobile towers are being installed for mobile connectivity. The inauguration of IIM and laying the foundation stone of Technology Park in Meghalaya will also expand the opportunities for education and earning. More than 150 Eklavya Model Schools are being set up in the tribal areas of the Northeast,[1] out of which 39 are in Meghalaya. In this budget, provision has also been made to recruit a large number of teachers in Eklavya Model Schools. Parvatmala Yojana will increase the convenience of tourist places here and tourism will also develop.

With regard to sports, the Central government is moving ahead with a new approach today, which has benefited the Northeast the most. The governments that were in the country for a long time had the idea of 'DIVIDE' for the Northeast, whereas Modi has come up with the idea of 'DEVINE'. Rejuvenation is happening with the DEVINE scheme. As Prime Minister Modi himself has said, 'We are removing all divisions between communities and regions, and in the Northeast, we are creating corridors of development, not borders of disputes.' In the last eight years, many organizations have left the path of violence and taken the path of permanent peace. Continuous efforts are being made to ensure that there is no need for Armed Forces Special Powers Act (AFSPA) in the Northeast. The decades-long border dispute between the states is being resolved. For us, the Northeast is not the end point, but the gateway to security and prosperity. Under Vibrant Border Village, emphasis is being laid on developing better facilities in the border villages. Tribal society has benefited the most from this policy of peace and development. The development of tribal areas is the priority while at the same time maintaining the tradition, language, food and culture of the tribal society. Bamboo was removed from the category of tree and brought into the category of grass. This gave a boost to the manufacture of tribal products associated with bamboo. Many Van Dhan Kendras have been established here. In Meghalaya, electricity has reached 2 lakh houses for the first time, more than 70 thousand houses have been built for the poor, 3 lakh families have the facility of tap water for the first time.

16

Punjab at Crossroads

Prime Minister Narendra Modi addressing virtually a semiconductor conference in Bengaluru

The Aam Aadmi Party (AAP) came to power in Punjab by promising the moon. The Arvind Kejriwal-led political outfit has earned the tag of a party of freebies from economic commentators. The Punjab budget presented by Finance Minister Harpal Singh Cheema failed to stem the slide of the state to financial bankruptcy. Cheema tried his best to play to the gallery by proposing a budget of ₹196,462 crore, while stating that it's 26 more than ₹1,55,869 crore in the financial year 2022–23. The proposed expenditure expansion is not backed by revenue growth.

The AAP-led government is further pushing Punjab into debt by increased borrowings. Punjab is already deep into debt. The Reserve Bank of India in its report on the state of financial health of a few states has expressed concern at the prevailing situations. This is captured in the official data, as the revenue deficit has spiked from 1.99 per cent in 2022–23 to 3.32 per cent.[1] Consequently, fiscal deficit has zoomed from 3.78 per cent in 2022–23 to 4.98 per cent proposed for 2023–24 fiscal. The situation has further aggravated the financial situations of Punjab as the Goods and Services Tax (GST) collections remained at ₹19,000 crore against a target of ₹20,550 crore in the current fiscal. This accounts for a shortfall of ₹1,500 crores.

Punjab is yet to come out with an industrial policy as promised by the AAP government even while industrialists are visiting Uttar Pradesh and other states in search for alternative investment opportunities. Economic activities seek peace and tranquillity as a precondition. But the Punjab government's evident neglect of the law-and-order situation is clearly making negative impact on economic activities. This has clearly been captured by the state government missing out on achieving the targeted GST collections. The poor track record on the revenue front has been documented by the state budget. Against the target set by the state government of ₹95,378 crore in revenue receipts, Punjab could manage just a net of ₹93,563.21 crore. This is being bridged by additional borrowings.

The Central government has already flagged that Punjab's debt situation is worrisome. Independent economists have for years been calling for corrective measures. But the incumbent Punjab government is paying least regards to the well-being of the future generations of Punjab by pushing the state further into debt trap. The ability of the state agencies to collect revenue is under severe stress. This can be seen in the performance of the transport department. Punjab roadways could earn only ₹90 crore against a target of ₹335 crore set by the state government.[2] Similarly, urban development revenue is also short by ₹69 crore as the government could collect only ₹200 crores. The total debt of Punjab in 2022–23 fiscal was pegged at ₹31.12 lakh crore. Punjab's debt has now zoomed to an estimated ₹3.47 lakh crore.

The state debt is close to 180 per cent of the annual budget of Punjab.[3] This makes the financial situation scary for Punjab, and the state government may soon begin defaulting on its obligations while also compromising aspirations of the people to create assets in education and health for better prospects of the future generations of the state. Already, the youth in Punjab are battling extraordinary unemployment situation, making them vulnerable to falling victims to drug cartels and organized armed gangs. This is being reflected in the state of education as the state against the promise of enhancing 100 schools to the status of institutions of eminence has just added thirteen more, while actual work could take place only in the case of four schools in the last one year. It must be stressed that the AAP has been running the government in Punjab now for almost one year.

On the health front, the Punjab budget has made attempts to be clever by re-packaging the Central government's 'Ayushman Bharat Health and Wellness Centres' into 'Mohalla Clinics'. The state government is trying to misguide the people of the state. The status of Punjab being a debt-laden state has begun showing impact on several fronts. The state is not able to modernize the police. The organized armed gangs are equipped with automatic assault rifles.

The police seem unable to control the gangs, whose writ run large in the state. In a survey of 30.46 lakh beneficiaries in Punjab, conducted by the Department of Social Security, Women and Child Development, it was found that the number of beneficiaries dipped by a whopping 90,248.[4] The state government failed to undertake construction of houses for the economically weaker sections last year. But that has not stopped the AAP government from making a promise to build 10,000 houses in this fiscal year. The performance of the state government in environmental management, solid waste management and several other areas remains abysmal, making the state cut a sorry figure on the national stage.

Known as a sword arm and the breadbasket of the country, Punjab has always shown a path of development and prosperity through its vibrant and healthy culture to the rest of the world. But, over the past few years, the state has been facing severe problems, the pain of which every Punjabi is feeling. Ironically, these pressing problems are the result of maladministration and lack of political will and vision on the part of the ruling dispensation. The land of Gurus today is passing through difficult times.

Economic growth is in shambles, unemployment is sky-high, the agrarian sector is in the doldrums, farmers are committing suicides and are under the burden of debt traps while the state has been reeling under heavy debt.

The economy of Punjab has historically been agrarian. After Independence, the economy of Punjab got a boost in the form of the green revolution. It made Punjab the number one state as far as per capita income is concerned, and Punjab enjoyed this title for more than two decades. Ironically, this green revolution led to the lop-sided development of various regions, sectors and sections of society. Data over the last three decades beginning 1990 shows that the agricultural growth rate has been less in Punjab than in other parts of the country. As of today, Punjab is the 15th largest state economy in terms of GSDP and 16th in terms of per capita GSDP. Punjab has focused on rice and wheat cultivation and has not been able to diversify its agrarian sectors as well as its economy.

It could not take benefits of opening up of the economy in 1991, which had huge potential considering the economic prosperity of the state. Even the push given by either the green revolution or reforms of 1991 did not lead to any industrial or manufacturing or service industry in Punjab. It is a classic case where the economic benefits of one sector of agriculture could not trickle down to the other sectors.

Pertinently, in this regard, Haryana has taken the lead and service sector cities like Gurgaon and industrial centres like Sonipat have become hubs of business activities.

This lack of transition to either the industrial or service sector has been the main reason for unemployment as well as the emigration of youth to other countries for greener pasture and job opportunities. The public exchequer of Punjab is in the doldrums. As per a recent projection by the Comptroller and Auditor General of India (CAG), Punjab's public debt would double in the next five years. The CAG further states that Punjab is using its new borrowings to repay the earlier loans, leaving little for capital expenditure.

As per the data of NITI Aayog, Punjab's per capita income has slid to below the national average and its per capita capital expenditure is among the lowest in the country. At this stage, we need an overhaul of our agriculture sector. Crop diversification is a must and focusing on fruit crops as Himachal has been doing must be scrupulously done. In this regard, Punjab must develop a viable industrial policy tapping immense potential in tourism, agriculture-related industries, dairy, sugar and farming activities, etc. Evenly spread clusters of industries and linking them with the export market so as to increase the outreach of the industries should be the focus.

Also, we need to fully tap the foreign remittances sent by almost one-crore strong Punjabi diaspora.

Drug Menace

After winning its war against militancy, Punjab has now been facing a major internal threat in the form of drug trafficking. None of the three regions of Punjab, viz., the Malwa, Majha and Doaba, have remained immune from the scourge of drug trafficking. As a transit route for drug trafficking, Punjab has slowly become a victim of drug abuse, which has permeated deep into the sociopolitical fabric of Punjab.

As per the NCRB, Punjab recorded 11,654 cases under Narcotic Drugs and Psychotropic Substances (NDPS) Act 1985 in 2018, which is the second highest in the country and accounts for 19 per cent of all such cases registered countrywide. Punjab is adjacent to the Golden Crescent (area of Pakistan, Afghanistan and Iran), which is the largest opium-producer area of the world and shares a 553-km border with Pakistan. It has emerged as a destination as well as a transit point for drug smuggling from Afghanistan. As per one report, opium-based drugs such as heroin and poppy husk, cannabis and pharmaceutical sedatives are the most used narcotics in the state. Surprisingly, Punjab neither produces plant-based natural substances like opium, cannabis and their derivatives nor manufactures the precursor chemicals which are processed into synthetic and psychotropic drugs.

It means that all of the drugs in Punjab originate from outside the state through a supply network controlled by local, interstate and international drug traffickers. Further, as per one study, the young population has been the worst sufferers of this menace. Although contrabands have spread their tentacles in all parts, the scourge of drugs has been concentrated in certain localities, clusters and villages. The issue of drug menace has been an election issue but nothing concrete has been done in the last four years to eradicate its scourge. No concrete actions either to check the spread of drug trafficking or prevent its outreach to the youth have been taken either.

The state administration has miserably failed in either forming a viable policy or taking effective steps to stop the use of these drugs. The promises of ending this menace have been more political demagogy than any doable or actionable plans. The state needs a political will and must address the nexus of drug trafficking and money laundering and check illegal and anti-national activities. Also, strict enforcement of the law and hitting hard on traffickers is a must. Further, popular culture through songs that promote drug use should also be banned. A counter-narrative through the use of the popular singers of Punjab against the drugs must be built so as to save the youth from its impressions. We need a political will and also a counterculture to counter the drug menace.

Punjabis have been at the forefront of defending the nation from any foreign invasions and have also been the bread-earner of India. However, over the past few years, Punjab has seen many problems, which are the results of poor government and a bad administration. Ironically, these pressing problems are man-made and are the results of apathy and lack of will on the part of political dispensation instead of socio-cultural factors. The land of the Gurus and Panj-Aabs (land between rivers) is going through difficult and tough times.

The root cause of these problems is sluggish economic development which is giving rise to many accompanying problems. The other major problem spreading its tentacles and choking the populace, particularly the youth of Punjab, is drug-trafficking, which needs immediate solution. For addressing these problems, we must have a vision of Punjab which should work as a goal to be achieved by the use of collective efforts of people of Punjab and government in Punjab.

Reports and studies have given several accounts of the drug menace in Punjab. The magnitude of the drug addiction among the people in Punjab is mind-boggling. Drug abuse is prevalent extensively. People from all walks of life are being drawn into the cobweb of drug addictions. Punjab has been the bulwark of India. Since the time of recorded history, Punjab has been the soul of India. Punjab is divine. The name of the state itself reveals divinity – the place of five rivers. The fertile land of Punjab nursed the Indian civilization. The idea of India came from the land of Punjab. Punjab is a land of valour. Courage is in the DNA of the people of Punjab. Cowardice doesn't exist in the dictionary of Punjab. The bravery of the people of Punjab scared the world conqueror Alexander. Supreme courage and sacrifice of Punjab extinguished the Mughal flame in India. The glory of Punjab brought civilizational gains to the people living even in Afghanistan. Punjab, thus, is an envy of India's neighbours. Pakistan set its nefarious designs in Punjab. Pakistan's military designs were crushed on the battlefields. Still, Pakistan didn't mind its ways. Islamabad switched gears to proxy war. Terrorism was exported to Punjab. India defeated Pakistan even on the proxy battlefield. Now, Pakistan has resorted to a new warfare. Drugs are the new weapons of Pakistan. With drugs,

Pakistan wants to subdue the bravery of the people of Punjab. Pakistan has spread a vast tentacle to push drugs into Punjab. Drones are being used for peddling drugs. Cross-border smuggling of drugs is also rampant. Even the sea routes to push the drugs sourced from Afghanistan are being used. There is a syndicate of drug peddlers active in Punjab. The extent of challenge has overwhelmed the existing facilities of de-addiction centres. Families are shaken. The jails are crowded by drug peddlers. Hospitals are also overwhelmed. Stories of agonies chronicling broken households, financial stress, indebtedness of the rural people, deaths are commonplace. This calls for a national response. This is a social cause that must be the top agenda of all the stakeholders. The civil society must step up their resources to deal with the issue. Political parties too must own up the challenge. Social activists must counter the sociological and psychological aspects of the crisis. Religious leaders too have abundant duty to intervene and rescue the people. Social service drives the Bharatiya Janata Party. Politics for the BJP is the means to serve the people. *Sewa* (service) is the mantra of the BJP. In times of the COVID-19 pandemic, when the people faced hardships on account of the national lockdown, the BJP workers were on the street for sewa to ensure that none went hungry and there was no suffering. This has been ingrained in the DNA of the BJP workers. They don't need to be directed by the party leadership to respond to the social crisis. The BJP workers on their own step out. For them, the people in distress are the family members. The BJP will be launching a 'yatra' in Punjab to free the state from the clutches of drug menace. This is the duty of the BJP workers. Punjab cannot wait anymore. Time to crush the tentacles of drug menace and the cause cannot be postponed for another day anymore. The top leadership of the BJP has taken a call to launch the yatra against the drug menace in Punjab. Union Minister for Home Affairs Amit Shah will take part in the yatra. The BJP president Jagat Prakash Nadda will also take part in the yatra. Several top leaders of the BJP will walk alongside the people of Punjab to send out the message that the drug menace has to be crushed in the state. Under the leadership of Prime Minister Narendra Modi, the BJP has taken several causes. The Central government has come out with policy response to deal with the social challenges. Some of the northern states had very poor sex ratio in the 0–6 age groups. A few of the states had seen mushrooming of the ultrasound clinics. They had come up solely to meet the growing demand to kill the girl child in the fetus. PM Modi rose to the occasion and gave a clarion call to the nation with 'Beti Bachao, Beti Padhao'. Within a few years, the practice of killing the girl child is now mostly eliminated. Similar result was seen with the campaign of 'Swachchata Abhiyan'. Sanitation became the mantra of nation. This helped India in dealing with the COVID-19 pandemic effectively. Now, the BJP is taking out yatra to extinguish drug menace in Punjab. This is to rescue Punjab. Enemies of India can never succeed.

Sadly, till date no political party has come up with any Punjab vision as to what are the goals of government and what are specific steps, i.e., strategy to be taken to achieve those goals.

Nava Punjab

It is a vision to create a new Punjab. What kind of Punjab we want to make or create? Nava Punjab envisages reviving the real Punjab where prosperity, peace and cultural vibrancy are at its best. Where there is economic prosperity, which is spread over people instead of being in few hands. Let our economy and agriculture lead to sustainable methods of agriculture and living. Let Punjab be a leading industrial hub of the country. Let our Punjab regain its number one spot in economic indicators, such as per capita income, which it had for more than fifteen years. Let there be employment and enough job opportunities across all sectors, viz., agriculture, industry and service. It should include all classes, people and zones.

The policy of government should aim at promoting innovation, creativity and efficiency. Further, the aim of economic development should not be just getting economic benefits but should also aim at sustainable development where the resources of the state, human or economic is so used as not to compromise their goals of development for Punjab.

It should aim not only at raising the standard of living but the standard of life that no person has to settle in foreign lands in search of employment. Let our soil and agriculture be free from pesticides and harmful fertilizers. Let Punjab be free from drug abuse. Let Punjab be free from pollution. Goals of development for Punjab should aim at economic development with development ethos that becomes a mass movement and culture where every Punjabi should participate, and the benefits of this development should trickle down to everyone. It should aim not only at raising the standard of living but the standard of life. Development should be egalitarian, which should ensure all the three regions of Malwa, Doaba and Majha and should benefit the future generations.

For the above economic vision, some practical and concrete steps could be:

- To increase the per capita income of the farmers and aim at doubling the per capita income with 2021–22 as the base in five years.
- In agriculture, a culture of 'agripreneurs' may be developed, where farmers will use innovative methods and best practices world over to revive the agrarian sector.
- To take effective steps to diversify the crop pattern and encourage cash crops, fruit crops, floriculture, dairy farming, poultry, piggery and fish farming.
- To develop industrial hubs in various regions. Stress must be focused on agro-industries and small industries.
- Punjab has an IT and ITM. To attach TM and IIT and management and various institutes of technology with the industries of Punjab so as to develop best practices.
- Punjab has huge untapped potential for tourism. To develop tourism hubs and to promote the culture of homestay. There are unexplored tourism spots in Punjab which will be developed as eco-tourism spots like Doldbha in Hoshiarpur, Harike Pattan, etc. Punjab has a well-knit network of canals to develop canal tourism on the model of European counties.

- To have pucca roads connecting all the villages of Punjab.
- To develop IT and service-based cities like Gurgaon.
- To ensure 24x7 electricity for farmers and industry. To ensure 100 per cent electrification of all households.
- Improve the ease of doing business in Punjab.
- Improve the share of industry in Punjab's economy.
- The major exports of Punjab are of manufacturing of wearing apparel and textiles (53 per cent share), machinery and equipment (15 per cent), food products (13.1 per cent) and motor vehicles, trailers and semi-trailers (6.5 per cent share). The government should work to export agriculture products and increase their share in Punjab's export basket
- Skill development is another important area. Education curriculum is developed to ensure basic skills which can result in growth in labour productivity.

17

Modi's Budgets Have People as the Soul

Prime Minister Narendra Modi is being briefed by the UN climate change envoy John Kerry

The budgets presented by the Narendra Modi government have always accorded the highest priority to the interests of the people. While Nation First is the mantra of the Narendra Modi government, the people occupy the soul of the budgets presented by the Centre in the Lok Sabha, which have been hailed by experts, cutting across the diverse ideologies for truly being Bharat budgets.

The Union budget 2023–24 has been historic for India. The budget paved the way for the progress of every sector and every class. It was the budget of the golden age of independence that focused on all-inclusiveness and aimed to elevate the strong foundation of self-reliant India. Under the able leadership of Prime Minister Narendra Modi and Finance Minister Nirmala Sitharaman, the budget further gave a push to the mantra of *sabka saath, sabka vikas, sabka vishwas* and *sabka prayas*.

The annual budget is a statement of income and expenditure of the Union government for a fiscal year, i.e., 2022–23. It underlines the sources of income and areas of expenditure of the Central government. It also underlines the focus area of government's spending both in terms of specific areas as well as the class of citizens. We have to see the prevailing background while proposing this budget, which includes the ever-changing COVID-19 uncertainty, changing dynamics of global economy and fast-changing world situations. Despite having these constraints, this budget is a bold step towards people's budget and is progressive and growth-oriented. I am sure if you read the budget document, you will find some new words which were never ever found in traditional budgets, such as drones, green job, virtual and skill labs and so on. The aim, goal and vision of the 2022–23 budget is to make the economy robust, develop core sectors and put the high-growth trajectory with an overall aim of addressing all sections of society, specifically the weaker sections, the poor and the farmers.

In this sense, it is one of the most progressive budgets India has seen in the last two decades. It has touched positively all the areas of the Indian economy and population. As per the vision of PM, the emphasis of this budget was on agriculture sector. This budget aimed at doubling the income of the farmers. This pro-farmer and pro-peasant approach can be seen from the fact that an allotment of over ₹2.25 lakh crore has been made for MSP to be directly transferred in the accounts of farmers. It covers 163 lakh farmers and 1,208 lakh metric tonnes of wheat and paddy crops.

To develop agrarian infrastructure, a river link of Ken-Betwa has been aimed at with a whooping cost of ₹44.5 thousand crore which will change the destiny of the area and people, particularly farmers along these rivers. An emphasis on natural farming, which will benefit the farmers on the banks of the river Ganga in Uttarakhand, Uttar Pradesh, Jharkhand, Bihar, West Bengal, is sought to be promoted, besides cleaning the river Ganga.

Also, use of drones for various agricultural activities like spreading pesticides, land mapping and others shows that this budget aims at linking technology and digitalization with agriculture practices. For any economy to grow in the short, medium and long run, a sizeable investment is to be channelized into infrastructure. This is also known as core sector, which includes roads, housing and transportation and which has a potential to expand and grow economy.

If this budget can be defined in one sentence, it was an infrastructure budget. As per the PM, more infrastructure and more investments will lead to more growth and this more growth will lead to more jobs. The benefits of the growth will trickle down to the economy. PMAY (housing) has been allotted a stupendous budget of ₹48,000 crore besides aiming at completion of 80 lakh houses by 2023.[1] A grand ₹60,000 crore has been kept for safe drinking water for 3.8 crore houses. Multi-model national parks, 400 new generation trains, expansion of

25,000 km of national highway network, Vibrant Village Programmes, etc, are going to take Indian economy to a higher trajectory.

Further, exploiting the renewable energy sectors like increasing solar capacity, using biomass in thermal power plants (5.7 per cent pallets), are the other steps in this direction. In terms of human resources, the health of citizens is very significant. For this, national digital health ecosystems and tele-mental health programmes have been proposed. Through various schemes, special emphasis is laid on the health of women and children with increased budgetary outlays. For education, e-content with a special stress on quality e-content has been underlined. For increasing creativity and skill development, 750 virtual labs and 75 skilling labs have been aimed at by 2023. For digitalization, digital banking units, helping start-ups for Drone Shakti and various other steps have been taken. Enunciating a new paradigm in the traditional budgets, it has introduced a concept of 'green budget' like introducing sovereign green bonds, green job, etc, which aims at sustainable development whereby economic resources are developed in such a way as to benefit natural resources.

It is a people's friendly budget as it has addressed concerns of all the sections, all the regions, all classes with its special emphasis on the sectors and people who need special attention. It boosts spending towards growth-oriented policies that create jobs, boost manufacturing, help the agri-economy and aims at core infrastructure creation. It has been received well by all the sectors and people of the country, which is evident from the various economic-parameters and sentiments of the industry.

Union Budget and Defence

The geo-strategic location of India with such hostile neighbours necessitates that India should have an army which is modern, state-of-the-art and ready to fight and protect the borders of the country. We lost the 1962 war with China primarily because of ill preparedness and lack of state-of-the-art defence equipment. The defence of any country depends upon the professionalism, competitiveness and efficiency of its soldiers. Territorial integrity and defence of any country depend more on the morale and fitness of soldiers than on anything. If I tell you that 60 per cent of the budget of the Indian army goes to salary and pension and only 40 per cent is left for its capital and modernization, it will make you think that we are repeating the blunders of 1962 without learning any lessons from it.

The Modi government recently announced the historical structural reforms in the field of recruitment of army wherein personnel recruited under the Agnipath scheme are termed as Agniveers. Of the 45,000 to 50,000 recruited annually, 25 per cent will be absorbed into the army to continue for another fifteen years under permanent commission. Under the Agnipath scheme, non-officer cadre army personnel would be recruited on a short-term contractual basis. Out of the total recruited, 75 per cent leaving the service will be given a lump sum amount of 11.71 lakh (corpus built by 50 per cent contribution by government and 50 per cent by personnel and interest earned).

India witnessed protests for the sake of protesting any 'change' which the Modi government is trying to bring for short-term as well as long-term benefit of India. There is no logic or sanity in such protests. Burning trains, buses, public properties and other assets smack of the anti-national elements fuelling the protests and jeopardizing the much sought-after reforms. They are playing in the hands of anti-India forces undermining national security.

Can we think of a probable situation in which any of such protestors joining the Indian Army where discipline and protecting the national assets are prioritized over even personal life? The Agnipath system will have a new kind of recruitment compared to ongoing age-long procedures. There is a consensus among all the defence experts that India's defence needs an overhaul structural reform. It is a fact that the average age limit of the Indian army is higher than the global standards. This new scheme will bring about desired changes.

On an average, the career settlement of a youth happens at the age of 29–30. The Agniveer scheme will give you job-cum-skills starting at the age of seventeen. This will significantly reduce the average age of Indian soldiers from 32 to 24–26 years, which will manifest in the health of the Indian defence system. The Agniveers will get ₹30,000–45,000 per month as salary. At the age of seventeen, you are getting such a salary with other collateral benefits. They will get a preference in government jobs as announced by many states. Also, there will be 10 per cent reservation of posts in the home and defence ministries for Agniveers. This will considerably reduce the defence pension bill which eats up a lion's share of the defence budget.

The National Institute of Open Schooling has announced that it will provide special courses for the Agniveers associated with the project to get class 10th and 12th pass certificates. This certificate can be used for entering higher education across the country. It will bring about professionalism and competitiveness as the 25 per cent chosen will be the best of the lot in terms of skill, agility and fitness. The remaining 75 per cent will be a pool of trained, skilled and equipped men who are ready to face the world with all the required skills and knowledge. In the next eight years, 1,40,000 will be well trained for defence and can be utilized for the country in an emergency situation. It will create a pan-India regiment having an all-India complexion. The army is not an employment generating avenue. We join the army primarily to serve and protect the country and if need be make sacrifices for the country. When someone protests just for protesting, it is the worst kind of disservice to the country.

Prime Minister Narendra Modi is working on the policy of *sabka saath, sabka vikas, sabka vishwas* and *sabka prayas*. All-round and all-inclusive development has taken place in our government without any discrimination of caste, religion, class, sect and region. People have been developed through schemes like Ujjwala Yojana, Ayushman Bharat, PM Kisan Samman Nidhi, PM Awas Yojana, Jal-Jeevan Mission, Swachh Bharat Abhiyan, Social Security Scheme, Saubhagya Yojana, etc.

The Global Minority Report, which came out in December 2022, has acknowledged that India is the best country for minorities. The report says that the way there is a special provision in the Constitution of India for the cultural and educational promotion of minorities, such provision is not there in any other country. This is not just a report, but a story of faith and growth. In October 2021, PM Modi went to the Holy Vatican City, where he met His Holiness the Pope. Narendra Modi has also invited him to visit India. PM Modi himself admitted that this meeting left a deep impression on his mind. In this important meeting, the challenges before humanity were discussed, and it was agreed that the spirit of unity and harmony can lead to the welfare of all. India is moving forward in this sense and under the leadership of PM Narendra Modi, the empowerment of every citizen here is getting stronger.

18

Narendra Modi: Global Saviour against COVID-19

Prime Minister Narendra Modi visits the international media centre at Bharat Mandapam during the G20 Leaders' Summit in New Delhi

India during the coronavirus pandemic proved to be the physician, pharmacist and healer of the world.

However, the Western media called India's crisis and response to the pandemic as a humanitarian disaster. To prevent the spread of the virus, to fight negative publicity as well as to deliver key health infrastructure requirements like medicines, ventilators, PPE kits, etc., were some of the most important challenges posed by the pandemic.

Not only was Narendra Modi's leadership effective, tough and visionary, India's healthcare infrastructure proved to be the global panacea. From Brazil in Latin America to Caribbean Islands, all benefitted from the India's leadership during the pandemic. It also needed lockdown, which was decried by a section of the political parties, while proactive steps were taken to mitigate the outbreak of the virus. At the same time, necessary steps were taken to protect the migrant workers and the vulnerable sections of society. At the operational level, sections of society hit hard by the lockdown were provided immediate relief by the Modi government. Pradhan Mantri Garib Kalyan Anna Yojna proved to be the game changer, and it was hailed globally as the most effective intervention by the government to protect the people from the hardships of the economic disruptions caused by the pandemic.

The world was observing with suspicion and curiosity how the second most populous country in the world would tackle the pandemic. It was indeed a daunting task which needed a three-pronged strategy: awareness, prevention and curative steps. How the nation has sailed through the unprecedented crisis under the leadership of Prime Minister Narendra Modi was a history in the making. How India successfully fought this challenge and emerged with flying colours would surely be part of the syllabus of the top management schools like Oxford, Harvard and Stanford in future.

The nation has almost passed the storm of corona under the stewardship of the karmyogi prime minister. In his faith and reliance on 'Make in India', the PM not only saw modern allopathic medicine as a way to treat people but brought in the Ministry of AYUSH to play the role. This immunity mantra, well projected by the PM, soon became a buzzword which not only helped boost immunity among the masses but also created awareness about Ayurveda. The health infrastructure came into focus with the maximum attention to the preventive aspects of the health emergency like masks, hospitalization, PPE kits, ventilators and oxygen cylinders. Every resource of the nation was diverted to this cause. Simultaneously, Indian scientists were encouraged to develop a protocol and effective vaccines. On 26 January 2021, the USA reported 4,101 deaths and the UK reported 1,631 daily deaths.

Even with their highly developed health care infrastructure, the western world struggled to deal with the pandemic. But India was seen as a healer of the world, with preventive medicines like hydroxychloroquine or curative Remdesivir coming to the rescue of global humanity. As of today, with a team of 29,000 only, India was able to contain the spread of the virus and bring down daily caseloads. The cases were down from nearly 1 lakh in September 2020 to below 9,100 per day now, with active cases falling below 1,74,000 within a few months. The recovery rate was achieved at nearly 97 per cent, which was the highest among the most affected countries.

India's vaccine is not only safe and reliable but also cost-effective. India is heading for the largest vaccination drive in the history of mankind, wherein it vaccinated its 1.3

billion population. India followed its ethos of 'Vasudhev Kutumbakam', wherein it gave doses of Made in India vaccines to other countries. India already gifted vaccine doses to Bhutan, Maldives, Nepal, Bangladesh, Myanmar, Morocco, Brazil, Seychelles, etc.

While China was blamed as the spreader of the virus, the world hailed India as a healer. India has emerged as the physician of the world and has turned out to be the pharmacy of the world, which is not only nursing its own population but the entire world.

India – The New Global Vaidya (Physician)

Mankind is passing through a very difficult phase of its existence due to COVID-19. Most scholars consider this pandemic as the toughest challenge before humankind since the Second World War. It has already been more than three years since the virus was first reported in China, and since then it has spread to all the five continents, covering almost all the countries in the world. The challenges thrown up by the COVID pandemic are unprecedented. As per the initial reports and studies, the developing countries with high population density like India would bear the major brunt of the coronavirus pandemic considering its population density, weak health and medical infrastructure and other factors like poor hygiene, poverty and lack of resources to deal with this crisis.

Western media, particularly the BBC, was very vocal in raising its concern regarding the spread of the virus in India and was skeptical about steps taken by the present government to contain the virus. They called India's crisis and response of the government a humanitarian disaster. They were even suggesting doom's day for India and catastrophe following the peak of this virus in India. Some critics tried to undermine the government's response by alleging even suppression of the true figures of persons affected by the coronavirus. The response of government to prevent the spread of the virus as well as to deliver the key health infrastructure like medicines, ventilators, PPE kits, etc. were doubted. Not only India's health care infrastructure was questioned but even the well-timed and well-executed lockdown was doubted since 70 per cent of the rural population is dependent on agriculture and April and May were the harvesting season for their Rabi crops.

To deal with COVID-19 was a daunting task. The situation was more severe than a war-like situation where the countrymen and the world had to fight against an invisible enemy. It needed an effective, tough and visionary leadership that could take decisions to save the countrymen from the clutches of this fatal pandemic. It also needed pro-active steps and focused approach on the part of nation instead of just relying on the systematic methods and knee-jerk reactions. It also needed to instil a feeling of faith in the nation that together we could overcome this crisis. At operational level, countering the coronavirus needed a three-pronged strategy; awareness, prevention and curative aspects in case the virus affects our countrymen on a large scale.

Right from the beginning, the government was so pro-active that even before the very first case of COVID-19 was reported in India, almost every Indian was made aware about preventive steps for corona through the use of phone ringtones and other measures. In the very initial address to the nation, the PM went for lockdown with the message '*jaan hai toh jahan hai*' (you have life only if you survive). Lives of the citizens were given priority over anything else. On the economic front, a slew of measures were taken up to boost the reclining economy and also to give direct benefits to lakhs of poor labourers and needy citizens following the lockdown.

The only effective way to save humanity from the tentacles of the coronavirus was a vaccine. One is reminded of the incident of Lakshman Murcha from the epic *Ramayana*, where Lakshman fell unconscious after being hit by Meghnath and was in dire need of Sanjivani (medicine) to save his life. When everything was in gloom, Lord Hanuman, despite all the challenges of time and roadblocks, found and delivered the herb in time to save the dying Lakshman.

Credit must be given to Team India led by an able leader who encouraged Indian scientists to develop a vaccine in a race against time. The Indian vaccine is not only safe and reliable but also cost-effective.

Notes

Chapter 2: Modi's *Arthniti*

1 Ministry of Finance, 'GST Revenue Collection for April 2023 Highest Ever at 1.87 Lakh Crore,' 1 October 2020, https://pib.gov.in/PressReleasePage.aspx?PRID=1921186.

2 Ministry of Finance, 'Aatma Nirbhar Bharat Package – Progress So Far,' 25 September 2020, https://pib.gov.in/PressReleasePage.aspx?PRID=1660691.

3 NITI Aayog, 'Empowered Committee for PLI Scheme for Large-Scale Electronics Manufacturing Approves Incentives for Foxconn India and Padget Electronics,' 20 December 2022, https://pib.gov.in/PressReleseDetail.aspx?PRID=1885189.

4 Ministry of Commerce and Industry, 'India's Services Exports Sets a New Record at USD254.4 Billion in FY2021-22, Beats Previous High of USD 213.2 Billion in FY2019-20,' 4 May 2022, https://pib.gov.in/PressReleasePage.aspx?PRID=1822664#:~:text=in%20table%20below.,India's%20overall%20exports%20(i.e.%20Services%20and%20Merchandise)%20touched%20USD%20676.2,20%20and%202020%2D21%20respectively.

5 *The Economic Times*, 'India's Mobile Phone Exports to Jump 75% to $5.5 Billion In FY 2021-22: ICEA-ET Telecom,' 25 March 2022, https://telecom.economictimes.indiatimes.com/news/indias-mobile-phone-exports-to-jump-75-to-5-5-bn-in-fy2021-22-icea/90420555.

6 *The Economic Times*, 'FDI Inflow Hits All-Time High Of USD 83.57 Billion in FY 2021-22,' 21 May 2022, https://economictimes.indiatimes.com/news/economy/finance/fdi-inflow-hits-all-time-high-of-usd-83-57-billion-in-2021-22/articleshow/91688456.cms?from=mdr.

7 OCED, 'Foreign Direct Investment – FDI Flows: OECD Data,' 2023, https://data.oecd.org/fdi/fdi-flows.htm.
8 Ministry of Commerce and Industry, 'India Gets the Highest FDI Inflow of USD 83.57 Billion in FY 2021-22,' 20 May 2022,https://pib.gov.in/PressReleasePage.aspx?PRID=1826946.
9 *Mint*, India's Agriculture Products Exports Cross $ 50 Billion for FY 2022, 6 April 2022, https://www.livemint.com/news/india/indias-agriculture-products-exports-cross-50-billion-for-fy22-details-here-11649246758828.html.
10 *Deccan Herald*, India's rank in Ease of Doing Business Has Moved to 63 in 2019 from 77 in 2018, 29 January 2021,https://www.deccanherald.com/business/union-budget/indias-rank-in-ease-of-doing-business-has-moved-to-63-in-2019-from-77-in-2018-944908.html.
11 NDTV, 'Business News, Market Updates, Economy, Finance, Stock, BSE, NSE, Nifty – NDTV Profit,' https://www.ndtv.com/business/more-than-1-67-lakh-companies-registered-in-2021-22-nirmala-sitharaman 3044828#:~:text=Finance%20Minister%20Nirmala%20 Sitharaman%20on%20Tuesday%20said%20that%20the%20 Ministry,lakh%20companies%20had%20been%20registered.
12 *The Hindu*, 'Over 1500 Obsolete Acts to Be Repealed in Winter Parliament session: Rijiju,' 23 October 2022, https://www.thehindu.com/news/national/over-1500-obsolete-acts-to-be-repealed-in-winter-parliament-session-rijiju/article66046283.ece#:~:text=%E2%80%9CWe%20 (NDA%20government%20at%20the,%2C%E2%80%9D%20 the%20Union%20Minister%20said.
13 World bank, '2023: Logistics Performance Index (LPI),' https://lpi.worldbank.org/international/global.
14 *Hindustan Times*, 'GeM's value 'suitably placed' to surpass ₹1.7 lakh crore mark in FY 2023,' 8 February 2023, https://www.hindustantimes.com/india-news/gems-value-expected-to-surpass-rs-1-7-lakh-crore-mark-in-fy-2023-101675868431449.html.

15 Ministry of Rural Development, 'Shri Giriraj Singh Calls for Efficient Implementation and Monitoring of Rural Roads Development Works by State Governments,' 24 May 2022, https://pib.gov.in/PressReleaseIframePage.aspx?PRID=1827963.

16 *Live Mint*, 'New FY 2024 Highway Target Highest So Far,' 26 October 2023, https://www.livemint.com/news/india/new-fy24-highway-target-highest-so-far-11690823460656.html#:~:text=official%20cited%20above.-,Highway%20construction%20reached%20its%20peak%20in%20covid%20year%202020%2D21,to%20just%20about%2010%2C000%20km.

17 Ministry of Civil Aviation, 'Shri Jyotiraditya M. Scindia Enumerates Achievements of Ministry of Civil Aviation on Completion of Nine Years of "Seva, Sushashan and Gareeb Kalyan",' 7 June 2023, https://pib.gov.in/PressReleasePage.aspx?PRID=1930553#:~:text=Till%202014%2C%20only%2074%20airports,Greenfields%20airports%20have%20been%20operationalized.

18 *Live Mint*, 'India Now Holds World Record for Fastest Road Construction: Nitin Gadkari,' 26 October 2023, https://www.livemint.com/news/india/india-now-holds-world-record-for-fastest-road-construction-nitin-gadkari-11617355320236.html#:~:text=India%20now%20holds%20world%20record%20for%20fastest%20road%20construction.,the%20minister%20said%2C%20reported%20ANI.

19 *Business Today*, '"India holds world record for fastest road construction," says Nitin Gadkari,' 3 April 2021, https://www.businesstoday.in/latest/economy-politics/story/india-holds-world-record-for-fastest-road-construction-says-nitin-gadkari-292555-2021-04-03#:~:text=India%20now%20holds%20the%20world,inaugurating%20the%20Tedhi%20Pulia%20flyover.0.

20 *The Economic Times*, 'PM Gati Shakti: A Game Changer that Can Help India Achieve $20-trillion Economy Dream by

2040,' 15 July 2022, https://economictimes.indiatimes.com/news/economy/infrastructure/pm-gati-shakti-portal-a-game-changer-to-achieve-20-trillion-economy-by-2040/articleshow/92812108.cms?from=mdr.

21 *Live Mint*, 'Agriculture Budget Rose 5 Times in 9 Years to over ₹1.25 Lakh Crore: PM,' 24 February 2023, https://www.livemint.com/news/india/agriculture-budget-rose-5-times-in-9-years-to-over-rs-1-25-lakh-crore-pm-modi-11677226541709.html.

22 Cabinet Committee on Economic Affairs, 'Cabinet Approves Implementation of Pradhan Mantri Krishi Sinchayee Yojna for 2021-26,' 15 December 2021, https://pib.gov.in/PressReleasePage.aspx?PRID=1781719#:~:text=degraded%20lands%20to%20bring%20additional%202.5%20lakh%20hectar&text=The%20Cabinet%20Committee%20on%20Economic,93%2C068%20crore.

23 Union Budget 2018-19, 'Agriculture: Union Budget Promises MSP 50% above Cost Doesn't Define Which Cost,' 3 February 2018, https://indianexpress.com/article/business/budget/agriculture-budget-promises-msp-50-above-cost-doesnt-define-which-cost-5049635/.

24 AgriNews Network, 'FAO Hosts First-Ever Global Conference On Sustainable Livestock Transformation,' 27 September 2023, https://www.agrinewsnetwork.in/ann-agri-news.php?id=913.

25 Ministry of Chemicals and Fertilizers, 'Year-end Review of the Department of Fertilizers 2022,' 23 December 2022, https://pib.gov.in/PressReleasePage.aspx?PRID=1886054.

26 Ministry of Finance, 12 February 2021, https://financialservices.gov.in/sites/default/files/Website%20%20January%2C%202023-%20English.pdf .

27 Ministry of Agriculture and Farmers' Welfare, 'Union Agriculture Minister Shri Tomar Launches DigiClaim for Claim Disbursal through National Crop Insurance Portal,' 23 March 2023, https://www.pib.gov.in/PressReleasePage.aspx?PRID=1909895.

28 Ministry of Food Processing Industries, 'Mega Food Park,' 2021, https://www.mofpi.gov.in/Schemes/mega-food-parks.

29 Ministry of Agriculture and Farmers' Welfare, 'Agriculture Accelator Fund,' 24 March 2023, https://pib.gov.in/PressReleaseIframePage.aspx?PRID=1910359.

30 *Outlook India*, 'Modi Govt Disbursed 27 Crore Mudra Loans To Women: Home Minister Amit Shah,' 6 June 2023, https://www.outlookindia.com/national/modi-govt-disbursed-27-crore-mudra-loans-to-women-home-minister-amit-shah-news-292532.

31 Ministry of Commerce and Industries, 'More than 92,000 Entities Recognized as Start-Ups since Launch of Startup India,' 5 March 2023, https://pib.gov.in/PressReleasePage.aspx?PRID=1913977.

32 *Business Today*, 'India Has 115 Unicorns with a Cumulative Valuation of over $350 Billion,' 2 February 2023, https://www.businesstoday.in/entrepreneurship/news/story/india-has-115-unicorns-with-a-cumulative-valuation-of-over-350-billion-368670-2023-02-02.

33 *The Economic Times*, 'Over 6 Crore ITRs Filed for 2022-23 Fiscal,' 30 July 2023, https://economictimes.indiatimes.com/news/economy/indicators/over-6-crore-itrs-filed-for-2022-23-fiscal/articleshow/102249853.cms?from=mdr.

34 Ministry of Heavy Industries, '2435 e-buses Deployed across Various States/UTs under FAME India Scheme Phase-II,' 14 March 2023, https://pib.gov.in/PressReleasePage.aspx?PRID=1906790.

35 *Business Standard*, 'Mobile Data Price Down 95%, Revenue up 2.5 Times in 5 Years: Trai,' 22 August 2019, https://www.business-standard.com/article/pti-stories/mobile-data-price-down-by-95-but-revenue-up-2-5 times-in-5-yrs-trai 119082101291_1.html.

36 Ministry of Finance, 'Pradhan Mantri Jan Dhan Yojana (PMJDY) – National Mission for Financial Inclusion Completes Nine Years of Successful Implementation,' 28 August 2023, https://pib.gov.in/PressReleaseIframePage.aspx?PRID=1952793.

Chapter 3: Narendra Modi Delivers Solution-based G20

1 G20.org, 'New Delhi Leaders' Declaration Final Adoption,' 9–10 September 2023, https://www.g20.org/content/dam/gtwenty/gtwenty_new/document/G20-New-Delhi-Leaders-Declaration.pdf.

Chapter 4: Modi Doctrine for Global Good

1 The White House, 'Remarks by President Biden and Prime Minister Modi of the Republic of India in Joint Press Conference,' 22 June 2023, https://www.whitehouse.gov/briefing-room/speeches-remarks/2023/06/22/remarks-by-president-biden-and-prime-minister-modi-of-the-republic-of-india-in-joint-press-conference/.

2 Press Information Bureau, 'Guidelines for Resource Adequacy Planning Framework for India-reg,' 28 June 2023, https://static.pib.gov.in/WriteReadData/specificdocs/documents/2023/jun/doc2023619214201.pdf.

3 Ministry of External Affairs, 'Question No. 3915: India's Efforts for UNSC Permanent Seat,' 6 April 2023, https://mea.gov.in/rajya-sabha.htm?dtl/36464/QUESTION_NO3915_INDIAS_EFFORTS_FOR_UNSC_PERMANENT_SEAT#:~:text=As%20a%20measure%20of%20its,elections%20held%20in%20June%202020.

Chapter 5: India: A Global Anchor

1 *Live Mint*, 'Operation Kaveri: India Evacuates over 3,000 Citizens from Sudan,' 3 May 2023, https://www.livemint.com/news/world/operation-kaveri-india-evacuates-over-3-000-citizens-from-sudan-11683099723701.html.

2 Ministry of Defence, 'Indian Navy Completes "Operation Samudra Setu",' 8 July 2020, https://pib.gov.in/PressReleasePage.aspx?PRID=1637314.

3 Indian Air Force, 'Operation Rahat,' 2015, https://indianairforce.nic.in/op-rahat/.

4 Ministry of Health and Family Welfare, 'Dr Mansukh Mandaviya Asserts Government's Commitment towards Improving Access to Quality Education for the Younger Generation,' 15 December 2022, https://www.pib.gov.in/PressReleasePage.aspx?PRID=1883704#:~:text=Consequentially%2C%20we%20now%20have%20648,Government%20and%20293%20are%20Private.

5 Ministry of Chemicals and Fertilizers, 'Year-end Review of Department of Pharmaceuticals,' 22 December 2022, https://pib.gov.in/PressReleasePage.aspx?PRID=1885753.

Chapter 6: Modi and India First

1 *Business Standard*, 'Unemployment Rate Declines to 6.8% in January-March 2023: NSO Survey,' 29 May 2023, https://www.business-standard.com/economy/news/unemployment-rate-at-6-8-per-cent-in-january-march-2023-nso-survey-123052900843_1.html.

2 UNEP, 'Why the Global Fight to Tackle Food Waste Has Just Begun,' 26 September 2022, https://www.unep.org/news-and-stories/story/why-global-fight-tackle-food-waste-has-only-just-begun.

3 *The Times of India*, 'LED Bulb Scheme Has Saved ₹20,000 Crore in Household Power Bills: PM Modi,' 4 March 2022, https://timesofindia.indiatimes.com/business/india-business/led-bulb-scheme-has-saved-rs-20000-crore-in-household-power-bills-pm-modi/articleshow/89998092.cms.

4 Ministry of Agriculture and Farmers' Welfare, 'Union Cabinet Approves Minimum Support Prices (MSP) for Kharif Crops for Marketing Season 2023-24,' 7 June 2023, https://pib.gov.in/PressReleasePage.aspx?PRID=1930443.

Chapter 7: Farmers First for Modi

1 *The Hindu Business Line,* 'New Leave Encashment Limit of ₹25 Lakh for IT Exemption to Be Applicable from 1 April in Old, New Regimes,' 25 May 2023,

https://www.thehindubusinessline.com/economy/new-leave-encashment-limit-of-25-lakh-for-i-t-exemption-to-be-applicable-from-april-01-in-both-old-new-regime/article66891500.ece.

2 NDTV, 'PM Awas Yojana Outlay Increased by 66% to ₹79,000 Crore,' 1 February 2023, https://www.ndtv.com/business/budget-2023-nirmala-sitharaman-pm-awas-yojana-outlay-increased-by-66-to-rs-79-000-crore-3742707#:~:text=Finance%20Minister%20Nirmala%20Sitharaman%20today,to%20over%20%E2%82%B9%2079%2C000%20crores.

3 *The Times of India*, 'Punjab and Haryana Need to Diversify from Wheat and Paddy,' 7 January 2021, https://timesofindia.indiatimes.com/readersblog/opinion-world/punjab-and-haryana-need-to-diversify-from-wheat-and-paddy-28899/.

4 Punjab Economic Survey, Department of Finance, 10 March 2023, https://finance.punjab.gov.in/uploads/10Mar2023/Economic_Survey.pdf.

5 *India Today*, 'How Punjab's Economy Is Going the Sri Lanka Way,' 9 September 2022, https://www.indiatoday.in/opinion-columns/story/aam-aadmi-party-punjab-economy-sri-lanka-economic-crisis-1998229-2022-09-09.

6 The India Forum, 'A Fresh Spike in Farmer Suicides in Punjab,' 30 June 2022, https://www.theindiaforum.in/article/spike-farmer-suicides-punjab.

Chapter 9: Pain of Punjab

1 *The Indian Express*, 'Punjab Budget 2023: Debt Crosses ₹3 Lakh Crore Mark, Subsidies to Bleed Exchequer,' 11 March 2023, https://indianexpress.com/article/cities/chandigarh/punjab-budget-2023-debt-subsidies-8490200/#:~:text=The%20debt%20figure%2C%20pegged%20at,end%20of%20next%20financial%20year.

2 *The Tribune*, '28-yr-old Woman Mastermind behind ₹8.5-cr Heist,' 15 June 2023, https://www.tribuneindia.com/news/

ludhiana/28-yr-old-woman-mastermind-behind-8-5-cr-heist-517266.

3 Punjab Assembly, 27 June 2022, https://punjabassembly.nic.in/images/docs/Budget_Speech_English.pdf.

Chapter 13: Narendra Modi: India's Foremost Cultural Ambassador

1 Ministry of Science and Technology, '231 Stolen Antiques Brought Back to India in the Last 9 years, Says Union Minister Dr Jitendra Singh,' 20 May 2023, https://pib.gov.in/PressReleaseIframePage.aspx?PRID=1925897#:~:text=Governments%2C%20he%20said.-,Dr.,the%20fast%20track%2C%20he%20added.

Chapter 14: Modi and Mahatma: Too Many Parallels

1 Prime Minister's Office, 17 September 2021, https://pib.gov.in/PressReleseDetailm.aspx?PRID=1884559.

Chapter 15: Narendra Modi: A True Punjabi with Love for the Northeast

1 *The Financial Express*, 'Setting a Record, India Administers over 2,26 Crore Vaccine Doses on PM Modi's Birthday,' 17 September 2021, https://www.financialexpress.com/lifestyle/health/setting-a-record-india-administers-over-2-26-crore-vaccine-doses-on-pm-modis-birthday/2332602/.

Chapter 16: Punjab at Crossroads

1 PRS Legislative Analysis, 'Punjab Budget Analysis 2023-24,' 10 March 2023, https://prsindia.org/budgets/states/punjab-budget-analysis-2023-24.

2 *The Indian Express*, 'Most Revenue Receipts Better than Last Fiscal but Fall Short of Target,' 11 March 2023, https://indianexpress.com/article/cities/chandigarh/punjab-budget-revenue-receipts-8490253/.

3 *Outlook India*, 'AAP in Punjab: Free Power, Higher Pensions and Excess Debt,' 20 June 2023, https://www.outlookindia.

com/national/aap-in-punjab-free-power-higher-pensions-and-excess-debt-news-296255#:~:text=Punjab's%20debt%20is%20almost%20180,down%20funding%20for%20the%20state.

4 *The Economic Times*, 'Punjab: 90,248 Deceased Beneficiaries of Pension Scheme Identified,' 27 October 2022, https://economictimes.indiatimes.com/news/india/punjab-90248-deceased-beneficiaries-of-pension-schemes-identified/articleshow/95129051.cms?from=mdr.

Chapter 17: Modi's Budgets Have People as the Soul

1 Moneycontrol, 'Budget 2023: Affordable Housing Gets Push, PMAY Allocated ₹79,000 Crore,' 1 February 2023, https://www.moneycontrol.com/news/business/real-estate/budget-2023-affordable-housing-gets-push-pmay-allocated-rs-79000-crore-9920551.html.

About the Author

Tarun Chugh is one of India's leading politicians. He is currently serving his second term as the national general secretary of the Bharatiya Janata Party. Chugh is also the party in-charge of Jammu and Kashmir, Ladakh, and Telangana, besides being a mentor to the youth wing of the party. He is an erudite politician and a leading debater in the political space in India. He takes a keen interest in literature and art.

Chugh hails from Amritsar in Punjab. He shot to national limelight in 1999 after taking out a 2,100-km-long Yuva Chetna Yatra to awaken the youth to national duty. Chugh has risen through the ranks of the BJP from the grassroots. He is a nationalist at heart and aspires to see India emerge as an economic superpower. Chugh has been actively involved in mentoring youths and students by overseeing training programmes to groom future leaders of the country.